Tuttle's Touches

S0-D0O-730

by MaryJo Tuttle

Dedication:

I'd like to dedicate this book to the men in my life. To my Husband, John, my best friend, best salesman, and best woodcarver ever. To our Son, Josef, my best critic, best color man, and patient computer wizard. To my Dad, Joe, for always letting me be a "Princess" and being proud of me. And in memory of, my Great Grandfather Howard, who taught me to dance in the living room to American Bandstand, my Grandfather Vernon, who taught me patience by taking me fishing, my Uncle Bub, who liked what I did, but never understood why people paid money for it, and my father-in-law Red, who taught me that a fender can't be fixed in a day and other valuable car facts, and who always took an interest in this painting thing.

Special Thanks:

Thanks to the men I work for and with, Bob for giving me the best job a painter could ask for, Don for being the best and most patient boss, and to Vince for keeping my wood stash well stocked.

Tuttle's Touches
MaryJo Tuttle
4300 Washington St • Vancouver, WA 98660
(360) 694-2886 • Fax (360) 693-3188 • Email: tolep8r@hei.net

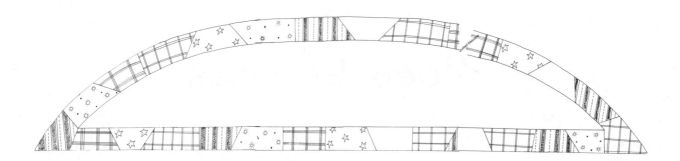

General Painting Instructions

Wood Prep:
All wood will need sanding. Be sure to sand with the grain of the wood. Remove the sanding dust with a dampened paper towel. Seal the wood, and sand again. I use Super Film Sanding Sheet for a final smooth surface sanding - I don't know how it works, but like what it does.

Basecoat:
The basecoat is the initial coat of paint on your surface. A thinner first coat, followed by a second will usually do the job. Don't rush this step, and use the biggest brush you feel comfortable with.

Shading/Highlighting:
I use a three brush method for this process. A large flat brush to dampen the surface, an angle shader to float color, and a mop brush to soften the color. For something to have shape, both sides need to have color, and the center must to be brighter. I use lots of center highlights in my painting, and the mop brush is a life saver!

Santa Beards
I use a filbert rake for the first layers of Santa beards. This brush is always a mystery, but it just works. Water down a puddle of paint, rinse the brush, get most of the moisture out, then go back to the puddle of paint and load it well, touch it to a paper towel to take some of the "wet" away, and with a very light touch, stroke the beard. This is the one brush that you can't take special care of - it works better as it wears.

Tracing and Transferring Patterns:
Trace patterns onto tracing paper, transfer the design to your surface with graphite paper (light for dark surfaces, dark for lighter surfaces), and a stylus. Transfer with a light touch so you don't carve the design into the wood. Graphite lines can be erased if you don't paint over them.

Brushes/Brush Care:
Your painting will be only as good as your brushes. Buy the best you can afford, and take care of them so they'll last. Never let a brush sit with paint in it, never let the brush sit in water, and wash the brush out often as you paint.

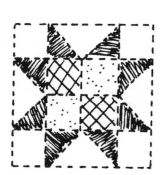  

Wood Sources

Cabin Crafters
1225 West First St
Nevada, IA 50201
800-669-3920
www.cabincrafters.com

Smooth Cut Wood
PO Box 507 A
Aurora, OR 97002
800-382-9663

Cupboard Distributing
1463 S. US Hwy 68
Urbana, OH 43078-8405
937-652-3388
www.cdwood.com

Wayne's Woodenware, Inc.
102C South Fieldcrest Drive
Neenah, WI 54956
800-840-1497
www.wayneswoodenware.com

the Artist's Club
PO Box 8930
Vancouver, WA 98668-8930
800-845-6507
www.artistsclub.com

Supply List

DecoArt Americana Paints
Antique Gold DA09
Antique Rose DA156
Antique Teal DA158
Antique White DA58
Avocado DA52
Baby Pink DA31
Black Green DA157
Black Plum DA172
Bluegrass Green DA47
Burnt Orange DA16
Burnt Sienna DA63
Burnt Umber DA64
Buttermilk DA03
Cadmium Yellow DA10
Camel DA191
Celery Green DA208
Country Red DA18
Deep Midnight Blue DA166
Desert Turquoise DA44
Fawn DA242
French Blue Grey DA98
Georgia Clay DA17
Gooseberry Pink DA27
Graphite DA161
Hauser Dark Green DA133
Hauser Light Green DA131
Hauser Medium Green DA132
Honey Brown DA163
Khaki Tan DA173
Lamp Black DA67
Leaf Green DA51
Light Avocado DA106
Light Buttermilk DA164
Light French Blue DA185
Marigold DA194
Medium Flesh DA102
Milk Chocolate DA174
Mississippi Mud DA94
Moon Yellow DA07
Napa Red DA165
Neutral Grey DA95
Pansy Lavender DA154
Payne's Grey DA167
Pumpkin DA13
Rookwood Red DA97
Shading Flesh DA137
Slate Grey DA68
Soft Black DA155
Titanium (Snow) White DA01
Uniform Blue DA86
Winter Blue DA190
Dazzling Metallics Emperor's Gold DA148
Hot Shots Fiery Red DHS4
Hot Shots Thermal Green DHS5
Hot Shots Torrid Orange DHS2

JW Etc Fruitwood Wood Stain
DecoArt Easy Float DS20
DecoArt Weathered Wood DAS8
DecoArt Multipurpose Sealer DS17

Kerry Trout's Liquid Shadow
Super Film Sanding Sheets
American Traditional Stencil MS121

Loew-Cornell Brushes
Angle Shader Series 7400, size 5/8"
Glaze Wash Series 7550, size 3/4"
Filbert Rake Series 7520, size 1/8" and 1/4"
Flat Shader Series 7300, size 2, 4, 8, 10, 12
Jackie Shaw Liner Series JS, size 1
Maxine Thomas Mop Series 270, size 3/4", 1/2", 3/8"
Debbie Mitchell Stipplers, size 1/4", 3/8"
Brush Basin II

Project Index

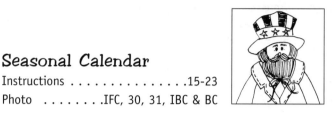

Seasonal Calendar

Santa. . . We've Got Cookies

Tall Red Box

Heart Candleholder with Holly

Quilted Christmas Coasters

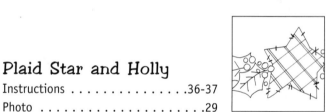

3 Faces of Santa Pins or Ornaments

Plaid Star and Holly

A Coat of Many Colors Santa

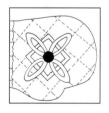

Heart Candleholder with Snowman

Quilted Mitten Ornaments

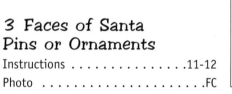

Quilted Stockings

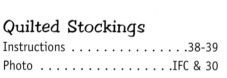

Project Index

Santa...We've Got Cookies

Palette:
DecoArt Americana Paints
Antique Rose
Avocado
Black Plum
Burnt Sienna
Burnt Umber
Buttermilk
Country Red
Fawn
Graphite
Hauser Dark Green
Hauser Light Green
Honey Brown
Lamp Black
Light Buttermilk
Marigold
Medium Flesh
Milk Chocolate
Neutral Grey
Rookwood Red
Shading Flesh
Titanium (Snow) White
Hot Shots Fiery Red

Misc. Supplies:
American Traditional Stencil MS121
Kerry Trout's Liquid Shadow

Prep:
Sand and seal bowl then sand again. Transfer main pattern lines and basecoat as follows:
Fawn - Background behind Santa and star blocks on rim (stars are Light Buttermilk)
Medium Flesh - Santa's face
Neutral Grey - Santa's hair, beard and mustache
Buttermilk - Santa's hat and sleeve cuffs, band where writing will go and holly blocks on rim (holly is Avocado, berries are Rookwood Red)
Avocado - Outside band and green blocks on rim (lines are Honey Brown & stitches are Rookwood Red)
Country Red - Santa's hat and suit
Honey Brown - Cookie and gold blocks on rim (large dots are Rookwood Red surrounded by smaller Hauser Dark Green dots, medium dots are Buttermilk)
Rookwood Red - Red blocks on the rim and outside of bowl

Painting Instructions:
Quilted Rim:
Highlight the centers and shade each side of the blocks around the rim as follows:
Red - Highlight Hot Shots Fiery Red, line plaid with Light Buttermilk, shade with Black Plum.
Green - Highlight with Hauser Light Green, shade with Hauser Dark Green.

Gold - Highlight with Marigold, shade with Burnt Sienna.
Tan - Highlight with Light Buttermilk, shade with Burnt Umber.
Holly Blocks - Shade with Milk Chocolate. Shade the base of the holly leaves with Hauser Dark Green and highlight the tips with Hauser Light Green. Shade the berries with Black Plum; highlight them with Hot Shots Fiery Red and a Light Buttermilk dot. Line the holly leaves and stitch between the blocks with Lamp Black. Shade around the outside of the bowl against the rim with Liquid Shadow.

Inside Bands:
Shade around both sides of the green band with Hauser Dark Green. Shade around the inside of the light band with Milk Chocolate and highlight the outside of it with Light Buttermilk. The words are lined with Rookwood Red. Shade around the outside of the star background and around Santa with Burnt Umber.

Santa: Shade Santa's face under the hat and above the nose with Shading Flesh. Blush the cheeks and bottom of nose with Antique Rose. Highlight the center of the face and top of nose with Light Buttermilk. The eyes are Lamp Black. The eyebrows are lined with Neutral Grey then Light Buttermilk. Highlight with dots of Light Buttermilk, upper right of eyes, top of cheeks and top of nose. Shade both sides of the hat and sleeve cuffs with Milk Chocolate and highlight the center with Light Buttermilk. Shade Santa's hat and suit with Black Plum, on hat above cuff, around the beard, both sides of the sleeves, above and below arms, and both sides and bottom of his tummy. Highlight with Hot Shots Fiery Red, center of hat, center of sleeves, and center of tummy. Highlight the mittens with Light Buttermilk. Shade all around the cookie with Burnt Sienna and highlight the center with Marigold. Add the chips in the cookie with Burnt Umber. Outline Santa and stitch between the bands with Lamp Black. Santa's hair, beard and mustache are lined with Light Buttermilk, and then Titanium White. Shade under the hat, under the nose and around the mustache with Graphite. Add more lines of Titanium White to break up the shade lines.

Finishing:
Varnish with your favorite product. If you're going to use this for cookies, I suggest a clear glass plate set inside.

Santa ......

We've Got Cookies

9

Heart Candleholder with Holly

Palette:
DecoArt Americana Paints
Antique White
Black Plum
Hauser Dark Green
Hauser Light Green
Hauser Medium Green
Lamp Black
Light Buttermilk
Milk Chocolate
Rookwood Red
Dazzling Metallic Emperor's Gold
Hot Shots Fiery Red
Hot Shots Thermal Green

Prep:
Sand and Seal Candleholder and basecoat surface with Antique White. Sand again with Super Film Sanding Sheet. Transfer the main painting lines and basecoat as follows:
Hauser Medium Green - Holly Leaves
Rookwood Red - Berries & outside edge of piece

Painting Instructions:
Shade one side of each quilting line in the background and around the edge with Milk Chocolate. Highlight the center of each section with Light Buttermilk. (I continued this quilting design onto the back side of the candleholder as well) Line stitches on the lines with Emperor's Gold. Shade around the design with Burnt Umber.

Shade the leaves with Hauser Dark Green at the base and vein line of each. Highlight the tips and opposite side of the vein lines of the leaves with Hauser Light Green, and then Hot Shots Thermal Green. The vein lines are stitched with lamp Black.

Shade the bottoms of the berries with Black Plum and highlight the tops with Hot Shots Fiery Red. Add a stroke and dot highlight on each berry with Light Buttermilk.

Finishing:
Outline the leaves and berries and add stitches around the outside with Lamp Black.

Varnish with your favorite spray or brush on varnish. Tie a string of raffia around a candle and enjoy. As with all candles, don't leave the candle burning unattended.

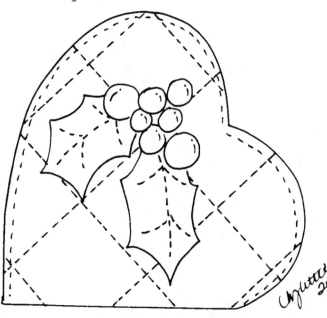

3 Faces of Santa-Pins or Ornaments

Palette:

DecoArt Americana Paints
Antique Rose
Antique White
Avocado
Black Plum
Burnt Sienna
Burnt Umber
Deep Midnight Blue
Graphite
Hauser Dark Green
Hauser Light Green
Honey Brown
Lamp Black
Light Buttermilk
Marigold
Medium Flesh
Milk Chocolate
Neutral Grey
Rookwood Red
Shading Flesh
Titanium (Snow) White
Dazzling Metallic Emperor's Gold
Hot Shots Fiery Red

Prep:

Seal pieces with DecoArt Multi Purpose Sealer, sand well and basecoat as follows:
Medium Flesh - faces
Neutral Grey - Beards on Heart & Santa shapes, and fur on Heart

Milk Chocolate - Beard and fur on Teardrop
Rookwood Red - Hat on Teardrop & # 1 patches on Heart
Avocado - #2 patches on Heart
Honey Brown - #3 patch on Heart
French Blue Grey - #4 patch on Heart (star is Light Buttermilk)

Painting Instructions:

Faces: Shade tops of faces and above noses with Shading Flesh. Highlight the center of the faces with Light Buttermilk. Blush the cheeks and bottom of noses with Antique Rose. The bald Santa has a kiss at the upper right of his head basecoated with Antique Rose - line between the lips with Rookwood Red.
Eyes are Lamp Black. Highlight upper right of eyes, top of cheeks and top of nose with small dots of Light Buttermilk. Undercoat the eyebrows with Neutral Grey and then line with Light Buttermilk.

Heart Santa:

Highlight the centers and shade the sides of the patches as follows:
#1 - Hot Shots Fiery Red / Black Plum
#2 - Hauser Light Green / Hauser Dark Green
#3 - Marigold / Burnt Sienna
#4 - Light Buttermilk / Deep Midnight Blue
The designs on the patches are as follows:
#1 - Lines are Light Buttermilk
#2 - Dots are Marigold
#3 - Lines are Lamp Black

11

Line the beard and then mustache using a Filbert Rake or Liner Brush with Light Buttermilk then Titanium White. Shade under the hat, nose and mustache with Graphite. Overstroke the mustache again with Titanium White. Stipple the fur with Light Buttermilk then Titanium White. Shade the outside edges and bottom of the fur with Graphite and then lightly stipple again with Titanium White.

Bald Santa:
Line the hair, beard and mustache using a Filbert Rake or Liner Brush with Light Buttermilk then Titanium White. Shade under the nose and mustache and at the peaks at the bottom with Graphite. Overstroke the mustache again with Titanium White.

Teardrop Santa:
Highlight the center of the hat with Hot Shots Fiery Red. The plaid is Emperor's Gold. Shade the hat above the fur with Black Plum.

Line the hair, beard and mustache using a Filbert Rake or Liner Brush with Antique White then Light Buttermilk. Shade under the hat, above the beard, under the nose and under the mustache with Milk Chocolate. Overstroke the mustache again with Light Buttermilk. Stipple the fur with Antique White then Light Buttermilk. Shade the outside edges and bottom of the fur with Milk Chocolate and then lightly stipple again with Light Buttermilk and then a little Emperor's Gold.

Finishing:
Varnish using your favorite product, glue a pin back or ribbon hanger to the back.

A Coat of Many Colors Santa

Palette:
DecoArt Americana Paints
Antique Rose
Antique Teal
Antique White
Black Plum
Blue Grass
Burnt Umber
Graphite
Honey Brown
Lamp Black
Light Buttermilk
Medium Flesh
Neutral Grey
Payne's Grey
Rookwood Red
Shading Flesh
Soft Black
Titanium (Snow) White
Uniform Blue
Hot Shots Fiery Red

Prep:
Sand and seal piece, transfer main pattern lines and basecoat as follows:
Medium Flesh - Santa's Face
Neutral Grey - Hair, beard and mustache
Antique White - Trim on hat, coat and hat tassel
Rookwood Red - Hat and coat
Antique Teal - Mittens
Lamp Black - Boots

The triangles on the trim are basecoated Honey Brown, Antique Teal, Rookwood Red and Uniform Blue

Painting Instructions:
Shade Santa's face under the hat and above the nose with Shading Flesh. Highlight the center of the face and top of the nose with Light Buttermilk. Blush the cheeks and bottom of the nose with Antique Rose. The eyes are Lamp Black. Highlight the eyes with a dot at the upper right and small stroke at the bottom left, and the top of the cheeks and nose with dots of Light Buttermilk.

Shade the top and bottom of the trim on the hat, sleeves and bottom of the coat, and both sides of the trim down the center front of the coat with Burnt Umber. Shade the left side of the hat trim, inside edge of the sleeve trim, under the beard on the trim, and both sides of the center front on the bottom trim with Soft Black. Highlight through the middle of all trim sections with Light Buttermilk. Line the tassel with Antique Teal, Uniform Blue, Rookwood Red and Honey Brown. Shade the top of the tassel with Soft Black. Outline each triangle with small stitches of Lamp Black. Shade the hat, above the band, outside and bottom of the tail, and in the dents, and the coat, under the beard, both sides of the sleeves, against the sleeves on the coat front, both sides of center front band, and above the trim at the bottom with Black Plum. Highlight the center of the hat, center of the tail of the hat, center of sleeves and center of coat fronts with Hot Shots Fiery Red.

Shade the mittens under the sleeves with Payne's Grey and highlight the tips of the mittens with Blue Grass. Highlight the boots with Neutral Grey, along the front and between them. The buttons are dots of Neutral Grey highlighted with small dots of Light Buttermilk. The stitches on the boots are Light Buttermilk.

Line the hair and then the beard and mustache with Light Buttermilk. Add more lines of Titanium White. Shade under the hat, above the beard, under the nose and under the mustache with Graphite. Add more lines of Titanium White to break up the shade lines.

Finishing:
Outline as necessary with Lamp Black. Varnish with your favorite product.

pattern for
A Coat of Many Colors Santa

Quilted Mitten Ornaments

Palette:
DecoArt Americana Paints
Antique White
Country Red
Hauser Dark Green
Lamp Black
Leaf Green
Light Buttermilk
Marigold
Milk Chocolate
Napa Red
Payne's Grey
Uniform Blue
Dazzling Metallic Emperor's Gold
Hot Shots Fiery Red
Hot Shots Thermal Green

Prep:
Sand and seal ornaments, transfer the line that divides the cuff and mitten, basecoat the mittens with Antique White, and one cuff Country Red, one Uniform Blue, and one Leaf Green. Lightly transfer the quilting lines to the mittens and shade the top of each line with Milk Chocolate (shade all in one direction, allow to dry and shade the other). Highlight the center of each square with Light Buttermilk. The stitches along the quilting lines are Emperor's Gold. Transfer the pattern for the design to each mitten and basecoat as follows:

Mitten with Red Cuff:
Uniform Blue - inside square
Leaf Green - line around blue square
Country Red - loops
Marigold - Button

Mitten with Blue Cuff:
Uniform Blue - center diamond
Leaf Green - ovals around center diamond
Country Red - outside ovals
Marigold - Button

Mitten with Green Cuff:
Leaf Green - small ovals
Country Red - large ovals
Uniform Blue - dots
Marigold - buttons

Painting Instructions:
Mitten with Red Cuff: Shade the cuff across the bottom and between the ribs with Napa Red, and highlight the opposite side of the ribs with Hot Shots Fiery Red. Shade the center of the blue square with Payne's Grey and highlight the outside with a brush mix of Uniform Blue + Light Buttermilk. Highlight the corners of the green stripe with Hot Shots Thermal Green. Shade the inside ends of the loops with Napa Red and highlight the outside ends with

Hot Shots Fiery Red. Shade around the design and under the cuff with Milk Chocolate.
Outline the bottom edge and between the ribs of the cuff and each part of the design with Lamp Black.

Mitten with Blue Cuff: Shade the cuff across the bottom and between the ribs with Payne's Grey, and highlight the opposite side of the ribs with a brush mix of Uniform Blue + Light Buttermilk. Shade the points of the diamond shape with Payne's Grey. Shade the bottom of the green ovals with Hauser Dark Green and highlight the tips with Hot Shots Thermal Green. Shade the bottom of the red ovals with Napa Red and highlight the tips with Hot Shots Fiery Red. Shade around the design and under the cuff with Milk Chocolate. Outline the bottom edge and between the ribs of the cuff and each part of the design with Lamp Black.

Mitten with Green Cuff: Shade the cuff across the bottom and between the ribs with Hauser Dark Green, and highlight the opposite side of the ribs with Hot Shots Thermal Green. Shade the bottom of the green ovals with Hauser Dark Green, and highlight the tips with Hot Shots Thermal Green. Shade the bottom of the red ovals with Napa Red, and highlight the tips with Hot Shots Fiery Red. Shade the inside of the dots with Payne's Grey and highlight the outside with a brush mix of Uniform Blue + Light Buttermilk. Shade around the design and under the cuff with Milk Chocolate. Outline the bottom edge and between the ribs of the cuff and each part of the design with Lamp Black.

Finishing:
Basecoat the back of the ornaments with Hauser Dark Green. Varnish with your favorite product. Thread a string through the buttons, tie a bow and glue the buttons to the center of the design on each mitten. Put strings through the holes for Hangers.

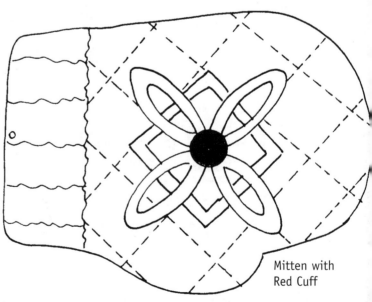

Mitten with
Red Cuff

14

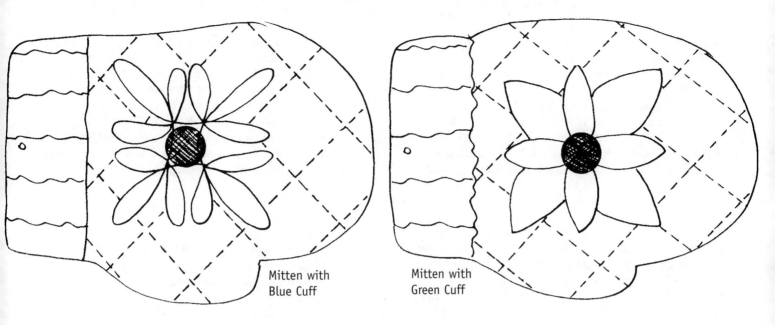

Mitten with
Blue Cuff

Mitten with
Green Cuff

Seasonal Calendar

Calendar Frame and Base:
Palette:
DecoArt Americana Paints
Antique White
Lamp Black
Milk Chocolate
Rookwood Red

Misc. Supplies:
Kerry Trout's Liquid Shadow
DecoArt Multi Purpose Sealer

Prep:
Sand and seal all wood pieces. Basecoat frame and base with Antique White.
Basecoat the bar and trim around the frame with Rookwood Red. Shade around the outside edge of the frame and base with Milk Chocolate. Shade around the bar using Liquid Shadow.

Finishing:
Varnish with your favorite product. Assemble the calendar by lining up the holes and sliding the brads into the holes and open them up to hold the pages in place. Set aside.

WINTER INSERT:
Palette:
DecoArt Americana Paints

Antique White
Burnt Orange
Burnt Umber
Deep Midnight Blue
Fawn
French Blue Grey
Graphite
Hauser Dark Green
Khaki Tan
Lamp Black

Light Buttermilk
Light French Blue
Marigold
Milk Chocolate
Payne's Grey
Rookwood Red
Slate Grey
Soft Black
Titanium (Snow) White
Uniform Blue
Hot Shots Fiery Red

Prep:
Sand and seal the insert, and basecoat with Fawn. Sand again with Super Film Sanding Sheet. Transfer the main painting lines and basecoat as follows:
Antique White - Snowman's face, hands & body, candle mittens on the bucket, and "T" block of the wall quilt
Slate Grey - Bucket, star & snowman's hat brim & cuffs
Light French Blue - "N" block and hangers on the wall quilt (plaid is Light Buttermilk) and #3 blocks on the outside of the table quilt.
Khaki Tan - Snowman's scarf & hat (lines are Rookwood Red, Lamp Black, and Light Buttermilk)
Rookwood Red - Snowman's coat, hearts & string on mittens on bucket, and sashing on table quilt
French Blue Grey - "W" and "E" blocks on the wall quilt (plaid is Light Buttermilk, Rookwood Red and Deep Midnight Blue) and #4 blocks on table quilt
Uniform Blue - "I" and "R" Blocks on the wall quilt (dots are Light Buttermilk) and #2 blocks on the table quilt
Deep Midnight Blue - Center and corner blocks of the table quilt (snowflakes are Light Buttermilk)
Light Buttermilk - #1 blocks on the table quilt

Painting Instructions:
Wall Quilt: Shade the "T" block on both sides with Milk Chocolate and highlight the center with Light Buttermilk. Shade the "N" block on both sides, and the bottom of the hangers with Deep Midnight Blue. Highlight the center of the block and tops of the hangers with Light Buttermilk. Shade the "W" and "E" blocks on both sides with Deep Midnight Blue and highlight the centers with Light French Blue. Shade the "I" and "R" blocks on both sides with Payne's Grey and highlight the centers with French Blue Grey. The stitches between the blocks and on the hangers are Lamp Black. Line the letters with Lamp Black with lines to the left of each with Light Buttermilk.

Snowman: Shade the snowman's face under the hat, hands under the cuffs and along the seam and body under the coat, down both sides and along the seam with Milk Chocolate. Highlight the center of the face, bottom of the hands and center of the body with Light Buttermilk. Blush the cheeks with Rookwood Red. The nose is Burnt Orange shaded at the base with Rookwood Red and highlighted at the tip with a touch of Marigold. The eyes and mouth are Lamp Black. Highlight with tiny Light Buttermilk dots at the top right of the eyes and top of the cheeks. The stitches on hands and body seams are Burnt Umber. The scarf and hat are shaded with Soft Black. On the hat, above the brim and down the left side of the tail; on the scarf both sides of the knot, bottom of the knot, next to the hat and on the ties, under the knot and down the right side of each. Highlight with Antique White, top of hat, center of tail, top of knot and center of each tie. Highlight the center of the sleeve and center fronts of the coat with Hot Shots Fiery Red. The plaid on the coat is lined with Lamp Black. Shade the coat with Soft Black, under the scarf, outside of left sleeve and above the cuff, under the hat on the right sleeve, down both sides of the coat, and to the right of the center front. Stipple the hat brim and cuffs with Light Buttermilk. Shade the hat brim on both sides and cuffs against the coat with Graphite. Stipple again in the center of the areas with Titanium White. Basecoat the jingle bell with Marigold, shade the bottom with Burnt Sienna and highlight the top with Light Buttermilk. The holes are lined and dotted with Lamp Black. The string above the bell is Antique White. Shade where it crosses over itself with Milk Chocolate and highlight the outside of the loops with Light Buttermilk. The buttons are large dots of Lamp Black. When dry, highlight the upper right of each with Light Buttermilk, and shade under each with Soft Black.

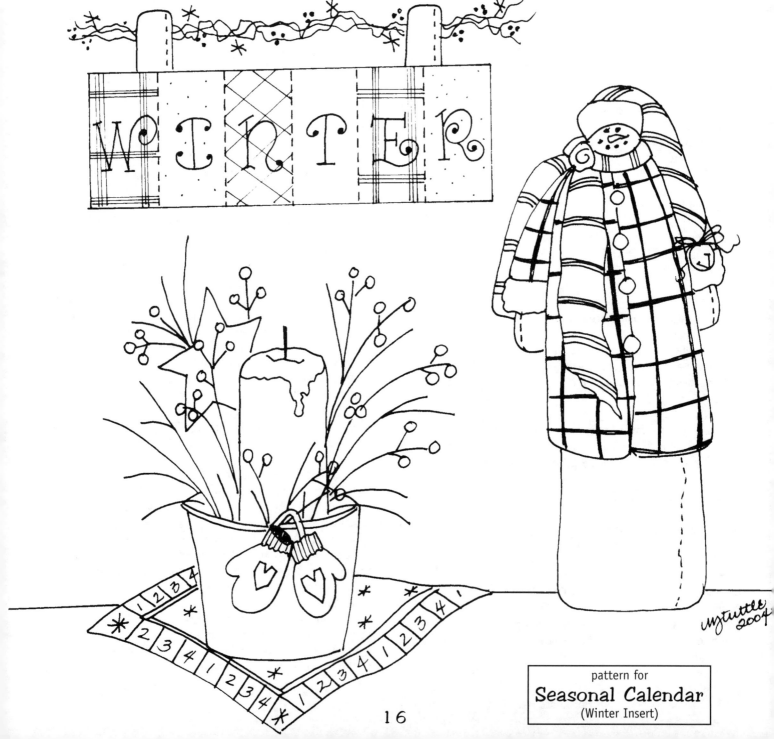

16

Table Quilt: Shade the red sashing at the ends and corners with Soft Black. Highlight the center of each sash with Hot Shots Fiery Red. Shade the blocks against the sashing with Payne's Grey and highlight the lower edge with Light Buttermilk. Shade under the bucket with Payne's Grey. Outline and add stitches between blocks with Lamp Black.

Candle: Shade down both sides, in the dent and under the drip with Burnt Umber. Deepen the shading in the dent and under the drip with Soft Black. Highlight the center of the candle and bottom of the drip with Light Buttermilk. Add the wick with Lamp Black and highlight the right side of the wick with a line of Light Buttermilk.

Star & Bucket: Stipple a little rust on the star and bucket with Burnt Sienna. Shade the star and bucket with Graphite, all around the outside of the star, inside, under the rim and down both sides of the bucket. Highlight the center of the star, center of the bucket and rim with Light Buttermilk.

Mittens: Shade the mittens with Milk Chocolate, inside left mitten, bottom of cuffs, down left sides and around thumbs. Highlight with Light Buttermilk, top of cuffs, bottom of thumbs, and bottom of mittens. Shade the string where it goes into the mittens and bottom of hearts with Soft Black. Highlight the top of the hearts and center of string with Hot Shots Fiery Red.

Background Shading: Slip the insert into the frame and with a chalk pencil draw a line around the frame on the insert. Remove insert. The background shading is done with Burnt Umber. Shade to the inside of your chalk line, around each object in the design and across the table line. Outline as necessary with Lamp Black.

Greenery & Vine: Line the stems in the bucket and vine holding the wall quilt with Burnt Umber. Deepen some of the stems and vine with Soft Black. The greenery is done with a #4 Flat Shader double loaded with Hauser Dark Green and Light Buttermilk. With the brush straight up and down, set it down on the branches with the green to the inside. Do each "needle" this way. Reload the brush often. The berries on the vine and on some of the branches are dots of Antique White. When dry, shade the bottom of the berries with Burnt Umber and highlight the tops with small dots of Light Buttermilk. The snowflakes on the vine are Titanium White.

Finishing:
Varnish with your favorite product. This insert is for January, February and some of March.

SPRING INSERT:
Palette:
DecoArt Americana Paints

Antique Gold	Graphite	Moon Yellow
Antique Rose	Hauser Dark Green	Rookwood Red
Black Plum	Hauser Light Green	Soft Black
Burnt Umber	Hauser Medium	Titanium (Snow)
Celery Green	Green	White
Fawn	Lamp Black	Hot Shots Fiery Red
Gooseberry Pink	Light Buttermilk	

Prep:
Sand and seal the insert, and basecoat with Fawn. Sand again with Super Film Sanding Sheet. Transfer the main painting lines and basecoat as follows:
Light Buttermilk - Bunny, pitcher and outside of table quilt
Moon Yellow - "P" and "N" blocks on wall quilt and bunny's dress (dots are Gooseberry Pink)
Celery Green - "S" and "I" blocks on the wall quilt, bunny's apron, and center of table quilt (double lines are Light Buttermilk)
Gooseberry Pink - "R" and "G" blocks and hanger on wall quilt, heart ends of table quilt and bunny's collar
Hauser Light Green - Tulip stems
Hauser Medium Green - Tulip leaves
Antique Rose - Tulips and sashing on quilt

Painting Instructions:
Wall Quilt: Shade the "P" and "N" blocks on both sides with Antique Gold and highlight the centers with Light Buttermilk. Shade the "S" and "I" blocks on both sides with Hauser Medium Green and highlight the centers with Light Buttermilk. Shade the "R" and "G" blocks on both sides and bottom of hangers with Antique Rose. Highlight the center of the blocks and the top of the hangers with a brush mix of Gooseberry Pink + Light Buttermilk. The letters are Hauser Medium Green. Shade the letters with Hauser Dark Green and highlight with Hauser Light Green. Line the left side of each letter with Lamp Black. The stitches between the blocks and hangers are Lamp Black.

Bunny: Shade the bunny with Fawn, left side of face, right side of left ear, left side of right ear, on the hands under the sleeves, on the legs under the dress and above the feet and bottom of the feet. Deepen the shading on the right ear and above the feet with Burnt Umber. Highlight with Titanium White, left side of left ear, right side of right ear, center of face, bottom of hands and center of feet. Blush the cheeks and bottom of ears and feet with Antique Rose. Basecoat the nose Antique Rose. Shade the bottom of the nose with Rookwood Red. Stitches on left ear, hands, legs and feet are Burnt Umber. The eyes and mouth line are Lamp Black. Place small highlight dots of Titanium White in the upper right of eyes, top of cheeks and right side of nose. Shade the dress with Antique Gold, above the apron on the bodice, on the sleeves next to the apron and above the gather lines, under the apron and down both sides of the skirt. Highlight with Light Buttermilk, center of bodice, center of sleeves, bottom of sleeves and bottom center of the dress. The stitches and bows at the sleeves are Antique Rose. Shade the collar with Antique Rose under the chin, and highlight the bottom with a brush mix of Gooseberry Pink + Light Buttermilk. The stitches on the collar are Light Buttermilk. Shade the apron with Hauser Medium Green, under the collar and down both sides. Highlight the center with Light Buttermilk. The buttons are Hauser Medium Green, shaded on the bottom with Hauser Dark Green and highlighted on the top with a small stroke of Light Buttermilk.

Table Quilt: Shade the center of the quilt and around and under the pitcher with Hauser Medium Green. Deepen the shading around the pitcher with Hauser Dark Green. Shade the light edge of the quilt against the sashing with Celery Green and highlight the "bumps" with Titanium White. Shade the sashing at the corners and point of the hearts with Antique Rose & highlight the bumps with Light Buttermilk. The dots are Gooseberry Pink with smaller Moon Yellow dots on top. The stitches between the outside sections are Lamp Black.

Pitcher: Shade the pitcher with Graphite, inside, under the rim, down both sides, top of handle and outside of handle. Highlight with Titanium White, center of rim, center of pitcher, top and bottom of handle.

Tulips: Shade the tulips with Rookwood Red, in the center, between the petals and bottom of petals. Deepen the shading in the very center with Black Plum. Highlight the

top of the petals with Hot Shots Fiery Red. Shade the stems under the tulips with Hauser Medium Green. Shade the leaves with Hauser Dark Green at the base and along the vein line and highlight with Hauser Light Green, at the tips and other side of the vein line.

Background Shading: Slip the insert into the frame and with a chalk pencil draw a line around the frame on the insert. Remove insert. The background shading is done with Burnt Umber. Shade to the inside of your chalk line, around each object in the design and across the table line. Outline as necessary with Lamp Black.

Vine: The vine holding the wall quilt is Burnt Umber. Deepen some of the vines and add tendrils with Soft Black.

18

pattern for
Seasonal Calendar
(Spring Insert)

Finishing:
Varnish with your favorite product. This insert is for part of March, April and May.

SUMMER INSERT:
Palette:
DecoArt Americana Paints

Antique Rose	Light Buttermilk
Burnt Sienna	Light French Blue
Burnt Umber	Marigold
Country Red	Medium Flesh
Deep Midnight Blue	Neutral Grey
Desert Turquoise	Payne's Grey
Fawn	Shading Flesh
French Blue Grey	Soft Black
Graphite	Titanium (Snow) White
Lamp Black	Dazzling Metallic Emperor's Gold
	Hot Shots Fiery Red

Prep:
Sand and seal the insert, and basecoat with Fawn. Sand again with Super Film Sanding Sheet. Transfer the main painting lines and basecoat as follows:
Light Buttermilk - "U" & "E" blocks on wall quilt (stripes are Country Red), light stripes on Sam's hat, Sam's pants (stripes are Country Red) and Sam's Shirt
Neutral Grey - Sam's hair, beard and mustache
French Blue Grey - "S" & "R" blocks on wall quilt and hatband (stars on both are Light Buttermilk)
Country Red - "M" block and hangers on wall quilt (dots are Deep Midnight Blue) and pot
Deep Midnight Blue - Sam's hat brim, coat, dowel holding wall quilt
Marigold - Stars at end of dowel
Lamp Black - Sam's Shoes

Painting Instructions:
Wall Quilt: Shade the "U" & "E" blocks on both sides with Soft Black, and highlight the center with Titanium White. The letters are French Blue Grey, shaded with Deep Midnight and highlighted with Light Buttermilk.
Shade the "S" & "R" blocks on both sides with Deep Midnight Blue and highlight the center with Light French Blue. The letters are Country Red shaded with Black Plum and highlighted with Hot Shots Fiery Red.
Shade the "M" block on both sides with Black Plum and highlight the center with Hot Shots Fiery Red. The letters are Deep Midnight Blue, shaded with Payne's Grey and highlighted with Desert Turquoise. Shade the hangers next to the quilt with Black Plum and highlight the top with Hot Shots Fiery Red. Line the left side of all letters, and add stitches between blocks and on hangers with Lamp Black. Shade the dowel with Payne's Grey, on each side of the hangers and against the stars. Highlight the center with Desert Turquoise. Basecoat the cut edge of the stars and shade the bottom of the stars with Burnt Sienna. Highlight the top of the stars with Light Buttermilk.

Uncle Sam: Shade Sam's face under the hat & above the nose, and on the hands under the sleeves with Shading Flesh.

Blush the cheeks and bottom of nose with Antique Rose. Highlight the center of the face, top of the nose and bottom of the hands with Light Buttermilk. The eyes are Lamp Black. Eyebrows, eye and nose highlights are Light Buttermilk. Shade the collar under the beard, the bottom of light stripes on the hat, on the pants under the coat and on both sides of the legs with Soft Black. Highlight the collar points, top of light stripes on the hat, and center of pant legs with Titanium White. Shade the bottom of the red stripes on the hat with Black Plum and highlight the top with Hot Shots Fiery Red. Shade the hatband on both sides, bottom of the hat brim, top of the lapel, under the lapel, both sides of the sleeves, both sides and down center of coat with Payne's Grey. Highlight the center of the hatband with Light Buttermilk. Highlight the top of hat brim, bottom of lapels, center of sleeves and center front of coat with Desert Turquoise. Highlight the top of Sam's shoes with French Blue Grey. Line Sam's hair, beard and mustache with Light Buttermilk, then Titanium White. Shade under the hat, under the nose, and under the mustache with Graphite. Line again with Titanium White to break up the shade line. The bow tie is Country Red, shaded with Black Plum and highlighted with Hot Shots Fiery Red. Add buttons on the center of the coat and sleeves with Emperor's Gold.

Flower Pot: Stipple the pot with Light Buttermilk. Shade the pot, inside, under the rim and down both sides with Black Plum. Highlight the center of the rim and center of the pot with Titanium White. Basecoat the stars on the front of the pot with Deep Midnight Blue, Country Red and French Blue Grey. The wire is lined with Lamp Black & highlighted with a line of Light Buttermilk in the center of each. Shade under each star on the pot with Soft Black. Shade the stars on the left and highlight the right as follows:
Deep Midnight Star - shade Payne's Grey/highlight Desert Turquoise
Country Red Star - shade Black Plum/highlight Hot Shots Fiery Red
French Blue Grey Star - shade Deep Midnight Blue/highlight Light Buttermilk

Line all of the stems and stroke small leaves in pot with Hauser Dark Green. Stipple under the white flower spikes with Light Buttermilk, and then do small 5 petal flowers with Light Buttermilk. Stipple under the red spike flowers with Country Red, and then do small 5 petal flowers with Country Red. Stipple under the blue flower spikes with Deep Midnight Blue, and then do small 5 petal flowers with French Blue Grey. Centers of all flowers are Marigold. The berries are dots of Country Red, Deep Midnight Blue and Light Ivory. Red ones are shaded on the bottom with Black Plum, blue are shaded on the bottom with Payne's Grey, and light ones are shaded on the bottom with Soft Black. All have Titanium White dot highlights. Shade again inside the pot over the stems with Soft Black.

Background Shading: Slip the insert into the frame and with a chalk pencil draw a line around the frame on the insert. Remove insert. The background shading is done with Burnt Umber. Shade to the inside of your chalk line, around each object in the design and across the table line. Outline as necessary with Lamp Black.

Finishing:

Varnish with your favorite product. This insert is for June, July and August.

FALL INSERT:

Palette:

DecoArt Americana Paints

Antique Gold	Georgia Clay	Pumpkin
Antique White	Graphite	Rookwood Red
Black Plum	Hauser Dark Green	Soft Black
Burnt Orange	Hauser Light Green	Dazzling Metallic
Burnt Sienna	Honey Brown	Emperor's Gold
Burnt Umber	Light Avocado	Hot Shots Thermal
Cadmium Yellow	Light Buttermilk	Green
Celery Green	Marigold	Hot Shots
Fawn	Neutral Grey	Torrid Orange

Prep:

Sand and seal the insert, and basecoat with Fawn. Sand again with Super Film Sanding Sheet. Transfer the main painting lines and basecoat as follows:

Fawn - End patches on wall quilt (leaves are Pumpkin)

Marigold - "F" patch on wall quilt (lines are Soft Black), center flower in can, and top patch on pumpkin stack

Emperor's Gold - Bands, handle, and top of spout on watering can

Burnt Orange - "A" patch, right flower and bottom of pumpkin stack

Light Avocado - First "L" patch on wall quilt (lines are Hauser Dark Green), hangers on wall quilt and bottom patch on pumpkin stack (dots on both are Marigold), watering can, and leaves

Hauser Light Green - Bow on pumpkin stack (lines are Pumpkin)

Honey Brown - Second "L" patch on wall quilt (lines are Antique White) and left flower

Georgia Clay - Middle section of pumpkin stack

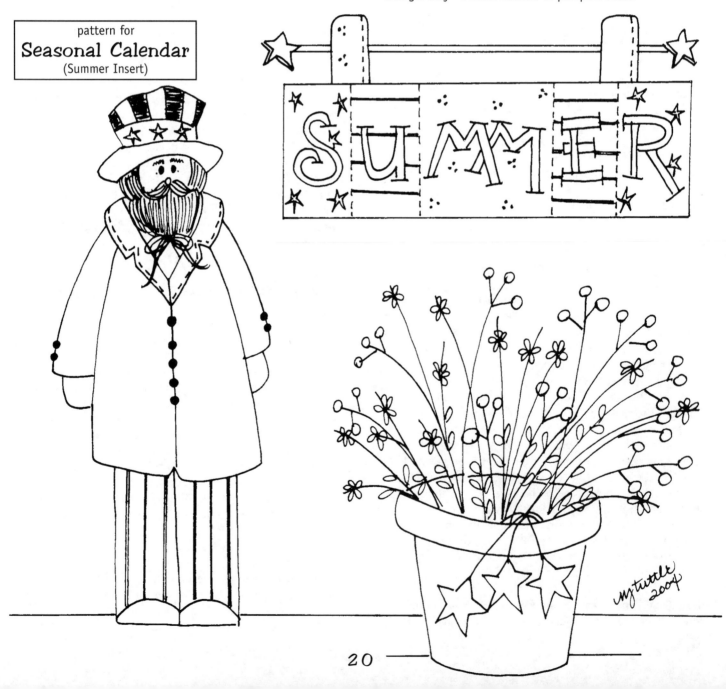

pattern for
Seasonal Calendar
(Summer Insert)

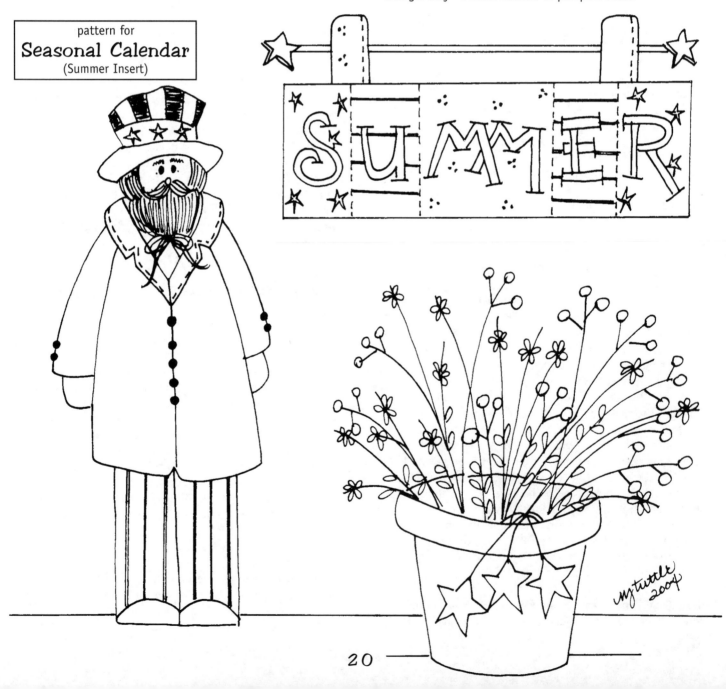

Pumpkin - Top section of pumpkin stack
Burnt Umber - Stem on pumpkin stack & flower centers (dots are L to R, Burnt Orange, Pumpkin, and Hauser Light Green)
Hauser Dark Green - Flower Stems

Painting Instructions:

Wall Quilt: Shade the end blocks on both sides with Burnt Umber. Shade the base of the leaves with Rookwood Red and highlight the tips with Hot Shots Torrid Orange. Outline and stitch the leaves with Lamp Black. Shade the "F" block on both sides with Burnt Sienna and highlight the center with Cadmium Yellow. Shade the "A" block on both sides with Rookwood Red and highlight the center with Hot Shots Torrid Orange. Shade the 1st "L" block on both sides and bottom of the hangers with Hauser Dark Green and highlight the center and top of the hangers with Hot Shots Thermal Green. Shade the 2nd "L" block on both sides with Burnt Sienna and highlight the center with Marigold. The letters are basecoated Soft Black and outlined with Lamp Black. The stitches between the blocks and on the hangers are Lamp Black.

Watering Can: Shade the green parts of the watering can with Hauser Dark Green - inside the can, front of can top, down both sides, both sides of spout. Highlight with Hot Shots Thermal Green - back of can top, center of spout and center of can. Shade the gold parts with Burnt Sienna - handle where it touches the can, bottom of spout, and both sides of the bands. Highlight the top of handle, front of spout and center of bands with Cadmium Yellow. Add holes to spout with Lamp Black dots. Shade the 2 yellow flowers at the bottom with Burnt Sienna and highlight the tops with Cadmium Yellow. Shade the bottom of the orange flower with Rookwood Red and highlight the top with Hot Shots Torrid Orange. Shade the base of the leaves with Hauser Dark Green and highlight the tips with Hot Shots Thermal Green. Shade the bottom of the flower centers with Soft Black. Stitches on leaves are Hauser Dark Green and stitches around flower centers are Lamp Black.

Pumpkin Stack: Shade the top pumpkin with Burnt Orange, outside edges, under the leaves and on both sides of the seam lines. Shade the middle pumpkin with Rookwood Red, outside edges, top under the bow, bottom, and both sides of

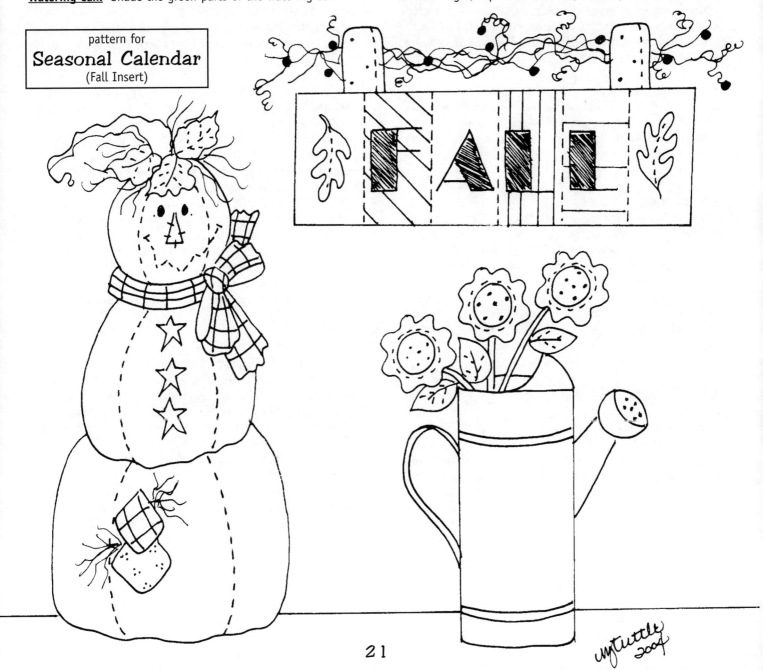

pattern for
Seasonal Calendar
(Fall Insert)

21

the seam lines. Deepen the shade on the outside of the seam lines and under the bow with Black Plum. Shade the bottom pumpkin with Rookwood Red, outside edges, top and bottom, both sides of seam lines and under the patches. Highlight each pumpkin with Hot Shots Torrid Orange, center sections and upper center of each outside section. The nose is basecoated with Rookwood Red, shaded on the bottom with Black Plum. The eyes, mouth line and stitches are Lamp Black. Highlight the eyes with small dots of Light Buttermilk. The stars on the middle pumpkin are basecoated with Neutral Grey. Stipple a little rust on each with Burnt Sienna. Shade the left side of each with Graphite and highlight each on the top with Light Buttermilk. Shade the top patch with Burnt Sienna on the bottom and highlight the top with Cadmium Yellow. Shade the bottom patch under the top patch with Hauser Dark Green. Highlight the right side with Hot Shots Thermal Green. Shade the stem with Soft Black and highlight with Marigold. Shade the base of the leaves with Hauser Dark Green and highlight the tips with Hot Shots Thermal Green. The vein lines are stitches of Hauser Dark Green. Shade the ribbon, both sides, inside the loops, under the knot, bottom of the knot, and under the loops with Hauser Dark Green. Highlight with Hot Shots Thermal Green, center, top of knot, ends of loops and end of ties.

Background Shading: Slip the insert into the frame and with a chalk pencil draw a line around the frame on the insert. Remove insert. The background shading is done with Burnt Umber. Shade to the inside of your chalk line, around each object in the design and across the table line. Outline as necessary with Lamp Black.

Finishing:

The straw at the top of the pumpkin stack and coming from the patches is lined with Burnt Sienna, Honey Brown and Marigold. Shade on the straw around the leaves and patches with Burnt Sienna. Add a few more lines of straw with Light Buttermilk. Add the tendrils with Lamp Black. The vine is lined with Burnt Umber. Deepen some of the lines and add some tendrils with Soft Black. The berries are Burnt Orange highlighted with small dots of Marigold. Varnish with your favorite product. This insert is for September, October and November.

CHRISTMAS INSERT:
Palette:
DecoArt Americana Paints

Antique Rose	Fawn	Payne's Grey
Antique Teal	Graphite	Rookwood Red
Antique White	Honey Brown	Shading Flesh
Black Plum	Lamp Black	Soft Black
Blue Grass	Leaf Green	Titanium (Snow)
Burnt Sienna	Light Buttermilk	White
Burnt Umber	Marigold	Uniform Blue
Cadmium Yellow	Medium Flesh	Hot Shots Fiery Red
Country Red	Milk Chocolate	Hot Shots
	Neutral Grey	Thermal Green

Prep:
Sand and seal the insert, and basecoat with Fawn. Sand again with Super Film Sanding Sheet. Transfer the main painting lines and basecoat as follows:

Antique White - End blocks on wall quilt & center of table quilt (trees are Leaf Green, trunks are Burnt Umber, and dots are Country Red), and trim on Santa's Suit (the triangles are Rookwood Red, Antique Teal, Honey Brown and Uniform Blue)

Country Red - Hearts on End blocks of wall quilt and #1 patches on table quilt

Light Buttermilk - "N" & "L" blocks on wall quilt (lines are Country Red)

Antique Teal - "O" block and hangers on wall quilt (dots are Light Buttermilk), balls on end of dowel, Santa's gloves & #2 blocks on table quilt

Rookwood Red - "E" block and dowel on wall quilt, #3 blocks on table quilt and Santa's suit

Medium Flesh - Santa's face

Neutral Grey - Santa's beard & mustache

Burnt Umber - Fur and ball on Santa's hat and trunk & branches of rag tree

Marigold - Star and pot

Painting Instructions:

Wall Quilt: Shade both sides of the end blocks with Milk Chocolate. Shade bottom of hearts with Black Plum and highlight the tops with Hot Shots Fiery Red. Shade both sides of the "N" & "L" blocks with Soft Black and highlight the centers with Titanium White. The "N" is Country Red and the "L" is Antique Teal. Shade "O" block on both sides and hangers next to the quilt with Payne's Grey and highlight the center of the block and top of hangers with Blue Grass. The "O" is Antique White. The "E" block is shaded on both sides with Black Plum and highlighted in the center with Hot Shots Fiery Red. The "E" is Light Buttermilk. All letters are lined in Lamp Black on the left side. Shade the dowel on both sides of the hangers and against the balls with Black Plum and highlight the center with Hot Shots Fiery Red. Shade the bottom of the balls with Payne's Grey and highlight the tops with Blue Grass. The stitches between the blocks, on the hangers, and blanket stitches around the hearts are Lamp Black.

Santa: Shade Santa's face under the hat and above the nose with Shading Flesh. Blush the cheeks and bottom of nose with Antique Rose. Highlight the center of the face and top of nose with Light Buttermilk. The eyes are Lamp Black. Eyebrows are Light Buttermilk. Add small highlight dots of Light Buttermilk in the upper right of eyes, top of cheeks and top of nose. Shade the suit trim with Soft Black, under the beard, both sides of the cuffs, under the mittens and both sides of the pant cuffs. Highlight through the center of the trim with Light Buttermilk. Outline each triangle on the trim with Lamp Black stitches. Shade the hat and suit with Black Plum, on hat above fur and ball, both sides of sleeves, both sides of the coat, both sides of pants and under coat. Highlight the top of hat, center of sleeves, center of coat front and center of pant legs with Hot Shots Fiery Red. Shade the mittens with Payne's Grey under the cuffs and highlight the tips with Blue Grass. Stipple the fur with Fawn then Antique White. Shade both sides of hat fur and bottom of ball with Burnt Umber. Stipple a little Light Buttermilk in center of hat fur and top of ball. Buttons are Honey Brown, shaded on the bottom with Burnt

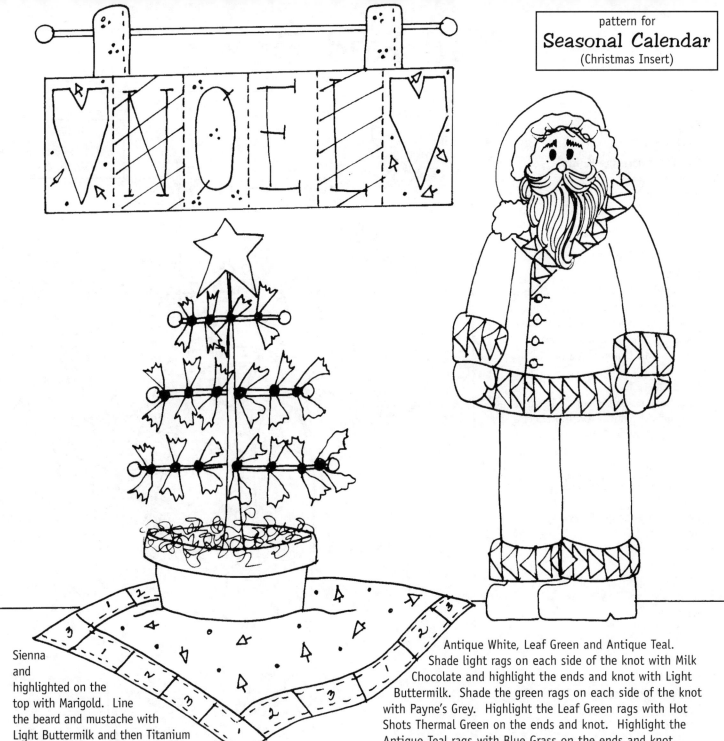

Sienna and highlighted on the top with Marigold. Line the beard and mustache with Light Buttermilk and then Titanium White. Shade under the nose and mustache with Graphite. Line again with Titanium White to break up the shade line.

Table Quilt: Shade the center of the quilt with Milk Chocolate across the top edge and under the pot. Highlight the front corner with Light Buttermilk. Shade all red blocks against the center with Black Plum and highlight the outside edge of red blocks with Hot Shots Fiery Red. Shade the green blocks with Payne's Grey against the center and highlight the outside edge with Blue Grass. The stitches are Antique White.

Tree: Shade the bottom of the star & pot, under the rim and down both sides with Burnt Sienna. Deepen shading on pot with Soft Black. Highlight the top of the star and center of the pot with Cadmium Yellow. Shade the tree trunk above and below each branch and on the ends with Soft Black. The rags on the branches are basecoated with

Antique White, Leaf Green and Antique Teal. Shade light rags on each side of the knot with Milk Chocolate and highlight the ends and knot with Light Buttermilk. Shade the green rags on each side of the knot with Payne's Grey. Highlight the Leaf Green rags with Hot Shots Thermal Green on the ends and knot. Highlight the Antique Teal rags with Blue Grass on the ends and knot. The dots at the end of each branch are Country Red, shaded next to the branch with Black Plum and highlighted on the outside with Hot Shots Fiery Red. Stipple inside the pot with Antique Teal, and then pull some squiggly lines of Antique Teal, and Antique Teal + Light Buttermilk.

Background Shading: Slip the insert into the frame and with a chalk pencil draw a line around the frame on the insert. Remove insert. The background shading is done with Burnt Umber. Shade to the inside of your chalk line, around each object in the design and across the table line. Outline as necessary with Lamp Black.

Finishing:
Varnish with your favorite product. This insert is for the month of December.

23

Tall Red Box

BOX:
Palette:
DecoArt Americana Paints
Rookwood Red
Misc. Supplies:
Kerry Trout's Liquid Shadow
Small knob for lid
Raffia

Prep:
Sand and seal box and lid and basecoat
with Rookwood Red. Sand again with
Super Film Sanding Sheet, and basecoat
a second time. Shade all edges and
corners with Liquid Shadow.

Finishing:
Add the knob to the top of the box and
varnish with your favorite product. Add
a string of raffia to the knob.

WINTER INSERT
Palette:
DecoArt Americana Paints
Antique Teal
Antique White
Black Plum
Burnt Orange
Burnt Sienna
Burnt Umber
Cadmium Yellow
Deep Midnight Blue
Desert Turquoise
French Blue Grey
Hauser Dark Green
Honey Brown
Lamp Black
Leaf Green
Light Buttermilk
Light French Blue
Marigold
Milk Chocolate
Payne's Grey
Rookwood Red
Soft Black
Hot Shots Fiery Red
Hot Shots Thermal Green

Prep:
Sand and seal insert and basecoat with
Light French Blue. Sand again with
Super Film Sanding Sheet, transfer main
painting lines and basecoat as follows:
Antique White - Snowman

pattern for
Tall Red Box
(Winter Insert)

French Blue Grey - Hat (lines are Deep Midnight Blue and stitches are Rookwood Red)
Rookwood Red - Hat and coat cuffs
Honey Brown - scarf (swirls are Rookwood Red, dots are Marigold)
Deep Midnight Blue - Coat (snowflakes are Light Buttermilk and buttons are Rookwood Red)
Burnt Umber - Tree trunks & branches

Painting Instructions:

Snowman: Shade face under hat, hands under cuffs and at seam line, and body under coat, down both sides and at seam line with Milk Chocolate. Highlight with Light Buttermilk, center of face, bottom of hands and center of body. The stitches are Burnt Umber. Blush the cheeks with Rookwood Red. Basecoat the nose with Burnt Orange and shade the base with Rookwood Red. Eyes and mouth are Lamp Black. Highlight eyes and cheeks with small dots of Light Buttermilk. Shade hat above cuff and both sides of tail with Deep Midnight Blue. Highlight the top of the hat and center of the tail with Light French Blue. Shade hat and sleeve cuffs on both sides and bottom of buttons with Black Plum. Highlight the center of the cuffs and top of the buttons with Hot Shots Fiery Red. Shade the scarf with Burnt Sienna, both sides, bottom of knot, under the knot on the ties and right side of both ties. Deepen the shading against the knot and under the knot with Soft Black. Highlight the center of scarf, top of knot and left side of ties with Marigold and then Cadmium Yellow. Shade the coat with Payne's Grey, under scarf, both sides and above cuff on sleeve, both sides and left center front. Highlight with Desert Turquoise, center of sleeve and center front of coat. Basecoat the jingle bell on the hat with Marigold, shade the bottom with Burnt Sienna and highlight the top with Cadmium Yellow. The hole is lined with Lamp Black. The string above the bell is lined with Antique White, shaded where it crosses over itself with Burnt Umber. Outline the snowman with Lamp Black.

Background Shading: Shade around the snowman and trees with Deep Midnight Blue.

Trees: Shade the left sides of the tree trunks and the branches where they touch the trunk with Soft Black. Add the rags to the branches with Antique White, Leaf Green, and Antique Teal. Shade the

light ones with Burnt Umber on both sides of the knot and highlight the ends and top of knot with Light Buttermilk. Shade the green ones with Payne's Grey on both sides of the knot and highlight the ends and top of knot with Hot Shots Thermal Green. The dots on the ends of the branches are Rookwood Red, shaded on the inside with Black Plum, highlighted on the end with Hot Shots Fiery Red. Add some Light Buttermilk highlight dots to the dots on the end and on some of the knots of the rags. Outline with Lamp Black.

Finishing:
Varnish with your favorite product.

pattern for
Tall Red Box
(Spring Insert)

25

SPRING INSERT:
Palette:
DecoArt Americana Paints
Antique Gold
Antique Rose
Avocado
Burnt Sienna
Celery Green
Hauser Dark Green
Hauser Light Green
Hauser Medium Green
Lamp Black
Light Buttermilk
Light French Blue
Medium Flesh
Mississippi Mud
Moon Yellow
Rookwood Red
Soft Black
Titanium (Snow) White
Hot Shots Fiery Red
Hot Shots Thermal Green

Prep:
Sand and seal insert and basecoat with Light French Blue. Sand again with Super Film Sanding Sheet, transfer main pattern lines and basecoat as follows:
Mississippi Mud - Ground
Medium Flesh - Face & Hands
Light Buttermilk - Collar, stockings and birdhouse
Celery Green - Dress (double lines are Light Buttermilk)
Moon Yellow - Apron
Antique Rose - Trim on apron
Burnt Sienna - Birdhouse roof and divider

Painting Instructions
Shade top of face, under chin, under sleeves and around thumbs with Shading Flesh. Highlight center of face, bottom of thumbs and hands with Light Buttermilk. Blush the cheeks with Antique Rose. The eyes are Lamp Black and mouth line is Antique Rose. Add dot highlights of Light Buttermilk to the top right of the eyes and top of cheeks. Shade the top and undersides of the collar, both sides and under the dress of the stockings, and the birdhouse under the roof and around the bottom with Soft Black. Highlight the points of the collar, center of the stockings and center of the birdhouse with Titanium White. The stitches on the collar are Lamp Black. Shade the dress under the collar on the bodice, under the collar and both sides of the sleeves and under the apron and both sides of the skirt with Hauser Medium Green. Highlight the bottom of the bodice, center of the sleeves and center of the skirt with Light Buttermilk. The buttons are Light Buttermilk shaded on the bottom with Soft Black and highlighted with at dot of Titanium White at the top. The apron is shaded with Antique Gold down both sides and highlight the center with Light Buttermilk. The trim on the apron is shaded with Rookwood Red under the collar and highlighted with Hot Shots Fiery Red at the bottom. The stitches are Antique Rose. The tie at the neck

is Hauser Medium Green shaded with Hauser Dark Green where it crosses over itself and highlighted on the loops with Hot Shots Thermal Green. Highlight the top of the shoes with Light French Blue. Transfer the tulip lines and basecoat the stems Hauser Light Green, the leaves Hauser Medium Green and the tulips Antique Rose. Shade the stems under the tulips and next to the thumb and base of the leaves with Hauser Dark Green. Highlight the tips of the leaves with Hot Shots Thermal Green. Shade the tulips with Rookwood Red, in the center and between the petals. Deepen the shade in the center with a second shade of Rookwood Red. Shade the ends of the birdhouse roof and divider and line the wire with Soft Black. Shade the ground with Burnt Umber and pull some grass using the 3 Hauser Greens.

Finishing:
The background shading is done with Deep Midnight Blue. The hair is lined with Antique Gold. Shade the loops at the base and where they cross over each other with Burnt Sienna. Highlight some of the loops with Moon Yellow. Outline with Lamp Black as necessary. Varnish with your favorite product.

SUMMER INSERT
Palette:
DecoArt Americana Paints
Antique White
Black Plum
Burnt Umber
Country Red
Desert Turquoise
Fawn
French Blue Grey
Honey Brown
Khaki Tan
Lamp Black
Light Buttermilk
Payne's Grey
Rookwood Red
Soft Black
Titanium (Snow) White
Hot Shots Fiery Red

Misc. Supplies:
DecoArt Weathered Wood
American Traditional Stencil MS 121

Prep:
Sand and seal the insert and basecoat with Fawn. Sand again with Super Film Sanding Sheet. Transfer the pattern line for the flag background and wash the field with Deep Midnight Blue, the light stripes and stars with Light Buttermilk, and the red stripes with Rookwood Red. When dry, basecoat the design as follows:
Deep Midnight Blue - Chicken body (stars are Light Buttermilk) and egg (apply Weathered Wood to egg)
Light Buttermilk - Chicken's head, medium tail feathers and egg

26

Rookwood Red - Large tail feathers and stick
Country Red - Comb and wattle
Khaki Tan - Small feathers between wing & tail
French Blue Grey - Wing
Honey Brown - Beak

Painting Instructions:

Shade both sides of the head, top and base of light tail feathers, and both sides of the egg with Burnt Umber. Highlight the center of the head, bottom of the tail feathers and center of the egg with Titanium White. The cheek is blushed with Country Red, the eye is Lamp Black, and both have dot highlights of Titanium White. Shade the beak next to the head with Soft Black. Shade the bottom of the comb, right side of the wattle, the red tail feathers around the light ones, and the stick under the chicken above & below the egg and above the base with Black Plum. Highlight the top of the comb, left side of the wattle, top and tips of the tail feathers, and center of the stick with Hot Shots Fiery Red. Shade the base of the feathers between the wing & tail with Burnt Umber. Highlight the tips of these feathers with Light Buttermilk. Shade the wing with Deep Midnight Blue and highlight the tip with Light Buttermilk. Shade around the body with Payne's Grey and highlight the center front with Desert Turquoise. Shade both sides of the base with Burnt Umber and highlight the center with Light Buttermilk.

Finishing:

The background shading is Soft Black. Outline the chicken and line the stitches on the flag in the background with Lamp Black. The raffia is lined with Antique White, shaded with Burnt Umber next to the knot and where it crosses over itself and highlighted on the loops and ends of ties with Light Buttermilk. Line with Lamp Black.

FALL INSERT
Palette:
DecoArt Americana Paints
Antique White
Burnt Orange
Burnt Sienna
Burnt Umber

Cadmium Yellow
Fawn
French Blue Grey
Graphite
Hauser Dark Green
Hauser Light Green
Hauser Medium Green
Honey Brown
Lamp Black
Light Buttermilk
Marigold
Milk Chocolate
Mississippi Mud
Payne's Grey
Rookwood Red
Soft Black
Uniform Blue
Hot Shots Thermal Green
Hot Shots Torrid Orange

Prep:

Sand and seal insert and basecoat
Fawn. Sand again with Super Film
Sanding Sheet, apply main pattern
lines and basecoat as follows:
Mississippi Mud - Ground
Antique White - Scarecrow's head
Burnt Orange - Hatband, shirt and
patch on knee (stripes on shirt and
patch are Rookwood Red, Light
Buttermilk and Hauser Light Green)
Uniform Blue - Pants
Hauser Light Green - Patch on hat and
pants
Soft Black - Hat and sunflower center
Milk Chocolate - Stick hands and legs
Graphite - Crow
Hauser Medium Green - Sunflower
stalk and leaves
Marigold - Sunflower petals

Painting Instructions:

Scarecrow: Shade the scarecrow's
head with Burnt Umber, under the hat,
above and below the gather line.
Highlight the center of the face and
bottom of the ruffle with Light
Buttermilk. Blush the cheeks and
basecoat the nose with Burnt Orange.
Shade the bottom of the nose with
Rookwood Red and highlight the top
with Hot Shots Torrid Orange. The
eyes, mouth stitches and the stitches
on the side of the head and bottom of
the ruffle are Soft Black. Highlight
the eyes and cheeks with dots of Light
Buttermilk. Shade both sides of the
hatband, the shirt under the head, in
front of the left sleeve, both sides of
the left sleeve and above the gather

line, both sides, above the gather line, and against the front
on the right sleeve and bottom of the patch on the knee
with Rookwood Red. Shade a second time with Rookwood
Red under the head and in front of the left sleeve.
Highlight the center of hatband, center of sleeves, center
front, and top of the patch with Hot Shots Torrid Orange.
Stitches at gather lines on sleeves are Lamp Black. Shade
the pants with Payne's Grey, above and below the rope tie,
down both sides of the legs, above the cuffs and under the
patches. Highlight the top of the pants, center of the pants
and center of both legs with French Blue Grey. Highlight
the top of the green patches with Hot Shots Thermal Green.
Add the plaid lines with Light Buttermilk. Shade the bottom
of the green patches with Hauser Dark Green. Line the rope
with Antique White. Shade with Burnt Umber at the back,

pattern for
Tall Red Box
(Fall Insert)

under the hand, and where the bow crosses over itself. Highlight with Light Buttermilk, top of knot, outside of loops and end of ties. Lines are Lamp Black. Shade the top of the hat brim and both sides of the top with Lamp Black. Highlight the bottom of the hat brim with Fawn. Shade the crow with Lamp Black, on the beak against the head, back of head, under wing and down the back. Highlight the front of head, bottom of wing, tummy and end of tail with Fawn. The eye is a dot of Light Buttermilk with a smaller dot of Lamp Black. The stick arms and legs are shaded with Soft Black and highlighted with Marigold. The grain lines are Lamp Black. The straw is lined with Burnt Sienna, Honey Brown, Marigold and Antique White. Shade where the straw touches the hat, patches, sleeves and pant legs with Burnt Sienna.

Sunflower: Shade the left side of the stalk, under the flower on the stalk, bottom of the leaves and above the vein line on the leaves with Hauser Dark Green. Highlight the tips of the leaves with Hot Shots Thermal Green. The petals are shaded with Burnt Sienna at the base of each, and highlighted on the tips with Cadmium Yellow. Shade the bottom of the center with Soft Black and highlight the top with Fawn. Add a few dots of Marigold. Shade the ground with Burnt Umber. Pull some grass with the 3 Hauser greens.

Finishing:
Background shading is Burnt Umber. Outline as necessary with Lamp Black. Varnish with your favorite product.

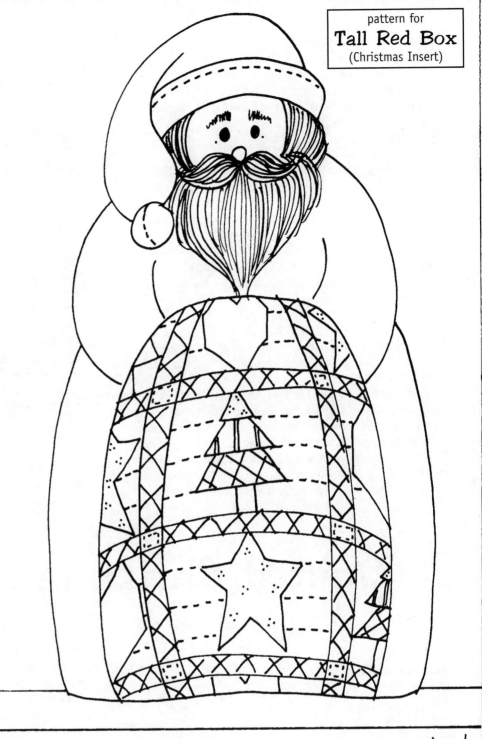

CHRISTMAS INSERT
Palette:
DecoArt Americana Paints

Antique Rose
Antique White
Black Green
Black Plum
Burnt Sienna
Burnt Umber
Country Red
Fawn
Graphite
Hauser Dark Green

Honey Brown
Lamp Black
Light Buttermilk
Marigold
Medium Flesh
Milk Chocolate
Neutral Grey
Rookwood Red
Shading Flesh
Titanium (Snow) White
Hot Shots Fiery Red

Misc. Supplies:
American Traditional Stencil MS121

Prep:
Sand and seal the insert and basecoat with Fawn. Sand again with Super Film Sanding Sheet. The stars are stenciled with Antique White.
Transfer the main pattern lines and basecoat as follows:
Medium Flesh - Santa's Face
Light Buttermilk - Hat cuff and ball
Antique White - Quilt Blocks
Rookwood Red - Santa's hat and suit and hearts on the quilt
Honey Brown -Stars on the quilt (dots are Marigold)
Fawn - Corner Squares on quilt
Hauser Dark Green - Quilt sashing, bottom sections of trees on quilt (plaid on both is Light Buttermilk)
Hauser Dark Green + Light Buttermilk - Middle section of trees on quilt (double lines are Light Buttermilk)
Hauser Dark Green + more Light Buttermilk - Top section of trees on quilt (dots are Light Buttermilk)

Painting Instructions:
Santa: Shade Santa's face under hat and above nose with Shading Flesh. Highlight the center of the face and top of nose with Light Buttermilk. Blush the cheeks and bottom of nose with Antique Rose. The eyes are Lamp Black. The eyebrows are lined with Neutral Grey and then Light Buttermilk. Add Light Buttermilk dot highlights to the top right of the eyes, top of cheeks and nose.
Shade the hat cuff on both sides and ball across the bottom and against the seam line with Burnt Umber. Highlight the center of the cuff and top of the ball with Titanium White. The stitches are Lamp Black.

Shade Santa's hat and suit with Black Plum, on hat above cuff and both sides of the tail, on the suit under the beard, both sides of the sleeves, against the sleeves on the chest, under the sleeves and against the quilt on the sides. Shade a second time above the hat cuff, under the beard, against the sleeves on the chest and under the sleeves with Black Plum. Highlight the top of the hat, center of the tail, center of the sleeves center of chest, and outside of suit with Hot Shots Fiery Red.
The beard is stroked with Light Buttermilk then Titanium White. Shade under the hat, above the beard, under the nose and under the mustache with Graphite. Stroke again with Titanium White to break up the shade line.

Quilt: Shade around the blocks and under each piece with Milk Chocolate. Highlight above each piece with Light Buttermilk. Shade the bottom of the hearts with Black Plum and highlight the tops with Hot Shots Fiery Red. Shade the bottom of the tree sections and ends of sashing pieces with Black Green. Highlight the top of the trees with Light Buttermilk and the centers of the sashing with Hauser Dark Green + Light Buttermilk. Shade the bottom of the stars with Burnt Sienna and highlight the tops with Marigold. The stitches are Lamp Black. Shade the bottom of the corner squares with Burnt Umber and highlight the tops with Light Buttermilk. The stitches on these are Light Buttermilk.

Finishing:
Background shading is Burnt Umber. Outline as necessary with Lamp Black. Varnish with your favorite product.

Quilted Christmas Coasters

Palette:
DecoArt Americana Paints
Antique White
Black Plum
Burnt Umber
Fawn
Hauser Dark Green
Hauser Light Green
Hauser Medium Green
Lamp Black
Light Buttermilk
Milk Chocolate
Payne's Grey
Rookwood Red
Dazzling Metallic Emperor's Gold
Hot Shots Fiery Red
Hot Shots Thermal Green

Prep:
Sand and seal, sand again with Super Film Sanding Sheet.
Basecoat the coaster holder as follows:

Antique White - back, sides and inside
Hauser Dark Green - front and bottom of bottom
Rookwood Red - cut edges and top of bottom
Transfer the pattern to the front of the holder and front and back of the coasters, and basecoat as follows:
Antique White - center and corners of the coasters
Fawn - star on holder and star points on quilt block
Hauser Medium Green - holly leaves on holder
Hauser Dark Green - one center square on the quilt block and two sides of sashing on both sides of coasters
Rookwood Red - one center square on the quilt block and two sides of sashing on both sides of the coasters

Painting Instructions:
Holder: Lightly transfer the quilting lines to the back of the holder and shade the top of each line with Milk Chocolate (shade all in one direction, allow to dry, and shade the other), also shade the outside and top edges with Milk Chocolate. Highlight the center of each square with Light Buttermilk. The stitches along the quilting lines and across the top of the front are Emperor's Gold.

pattern for
Quilted Christmas Coasters
(Coasters)

RED
GREEN
GREEN
RED

GREEN
RED
RED
GREEN

pattern for
Quilted Christmas Coasters
(Holder)

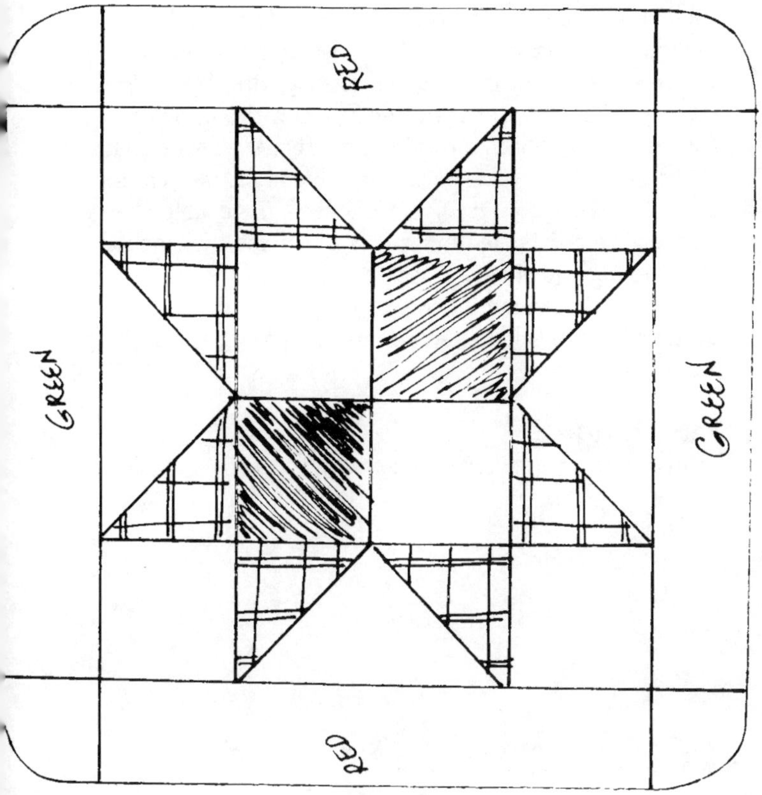

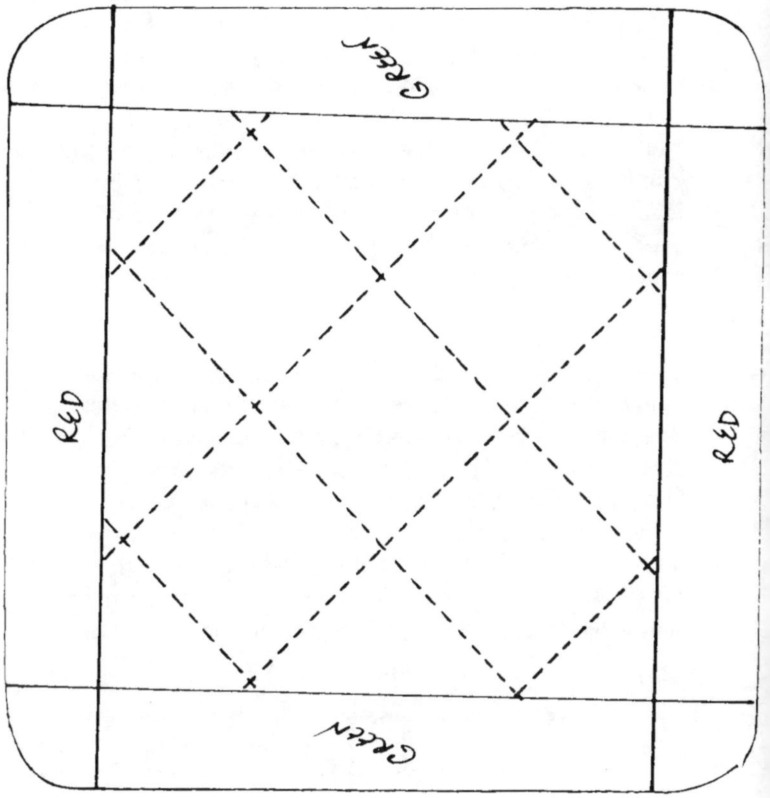

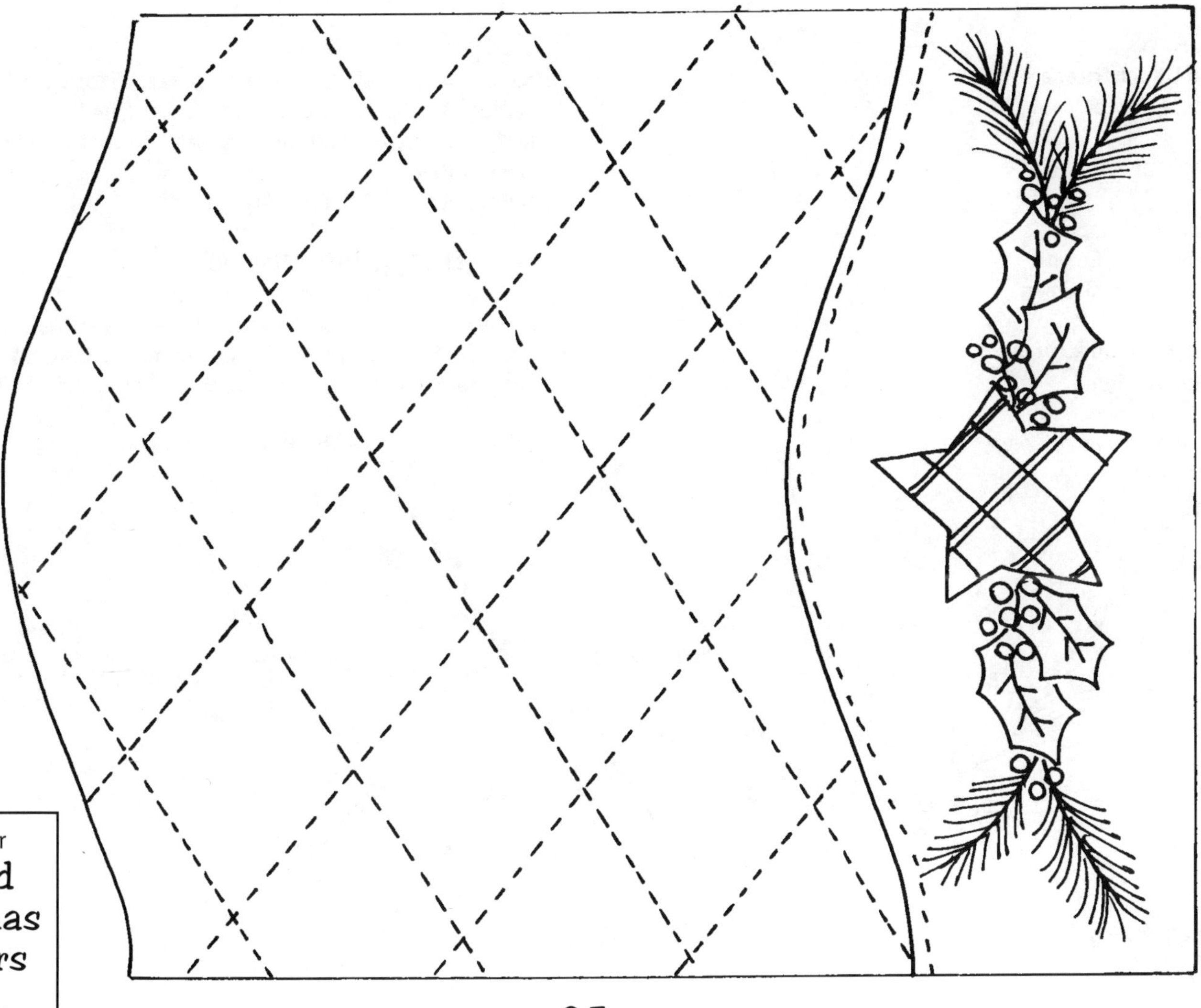

Highlight the center of the star with Light Buttermilk. The double plaid lines are Hauser Dark Green and the single plaid lines are Rookwood Red. Shade around the edge of the star with Burnt Umber. Outline and add crazy stitches with Lamp Black. Shade the base and bottom of the leaves with Hauser Dark Green and highlight the top and tips with Hauser Light Green and then Hot Shots Thermal Green. The vein lines are Hauser Dark Green. Outline with Lamp Black. Shade around the design with Payne's Grey. Line the fir boughs with Hauser Medium Green. Dot the berries with Rookwood Red. Add small Light Buttermilk dots to highlight the berries.

Back of Coasters: Lightly transfer the quilting lines to the center of the coaster. Shade the top of each line with Milk Chocolate (shade in one direction, allow to dry and shade the other), and highlight the center of the squares with Light Buttermilk. The stitches along the quilting lines are Emperor's Gold. Shade both ends of the red sashing with Black Plum. Shade both ends of the green sashing with Payne's Grey. Shade the inside corner of the corners with Milk Chocolate. The stitches around the sashing are Lamp Black.

Front of Coasters: Shade around the light squares and triangles, and the inside corner of the corners with Milk Chocolate. Highlight the centers of the squares and triangles with Light Buttermilk. Shade around the green square and the ends of the green sashing with Payne's Grey. Highlight the center of the green square with Hot Shots Thermal Green. Shade around the red square and the ends of the red sashing with Black Plum. Highlight the center of the red square with Hot Shots Fiery Red. The double plaid lines on the points are Hauser Dark Green and the single lines are Rookwood Red. Shade the inside of the triangles with Burnt Umber and highlight the tips with Light Buttermilk. The stitches around the quilt block and sashing are Lamp Black.

Finishing:
Varnish with your favorite product.

Plaid Star and Holly

Palette:
DecoArt Americana Paints
Antique White
Black Plum
Burnt Umber
Fawn
Hauser Dark Green
Hauser Light Green
Hauser Medium Green
Lamp Black
Light Buttermilk
Rookwood Red
Hot Shots Fiery Red
Hot Shots Thermal Green

Prep:
Sand and seal votive holder and basecoat surface with Antique White. Sand again with Super Film Sanding Sheet and transfer main pattern lines and basecoat as follows:
Fawn - star
Hauser Medium Green - holly leaves

Painting Instructions:
Highlight the center of the star with Light Buttermilk. The double plaid lines are Hauser Dark Green and the single plaid lines are Rookwood Red. Shade around the edge of the star with Burnt Umber. Outline and add crazy stitches with Lamp Black.
Shade the base and bottom of the leaves with Hauser Dark

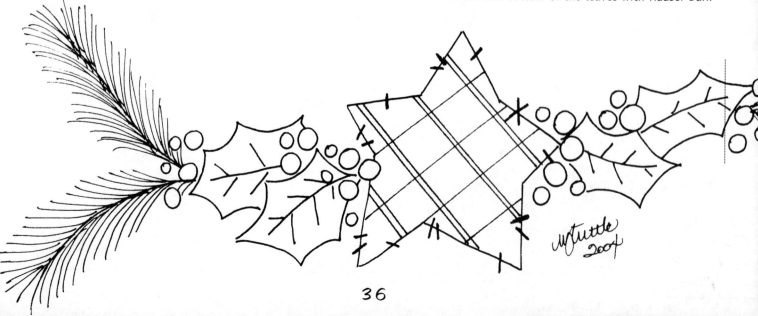

Green and highlight the top and tips with Hauser Light
Green and then Hot Shots Thermal Green. The vein lines are
Hauser Dark Green. Outline with Lamp Black.
Shade around the design and around the top, bottom and
sides of the votive holder with Burnt Umber.
Line the fir boughs with Hauser Dark Green, Hauser Medium
Green, Hauser Light Green and Light Buttermilk. Shade next
to the holly leaves on the boughs with Hauser Dark Green.
Basecoat the berries with Rookwood Red. Shade the bottom
of the berries with Black Plum and highlight the top with
Hot Shots Fiery Red. Add small Light Buttermilk dots on the
highlighted side of the berries.

Finishing:
Add dots of Hauser Dark Green in the background. Varnish
with your favorite product. Never leave a candle burning
unattended.

pattern for
**Plaid Star
and Holly**
(continued)

Heart Candleholder with Snowman

Palette:
DecoArt Americana Paints
Black Plum
Burnt Orange
Burnt Sienna
Deep Midnight Blue
Honey Brown
Lamp Black
Light Buttermilk
Marigold
Payne's Grey
Rookwood Red
Titanium (Snow) White
Hot Shots Fiery Red

Prep:
Sand and seal candleholder and basecoat surface with Deep
Midnight Blue.
Sand again with Super Film Sanding Sheet. Touch up
basecoat if necessary.
Transfer the main pattern lines and basecoat as follows:
Light Buttermilk - Stipple snowman
Honey Brown - Scarf
Rookwood Red - Stripes and heart on scarf

Painting Instructions:
Shade the snowman with Deep Midnight Blue, bottom of head,
under the scarf and down both sides of the body, arms against
the body and outside of thumbs. Highlight with Titanium
White, center of body, center of arms and center top of face.
Blush the cheeks with Rookwood Red. Basecoat the nose with
Burnt Orange. Shade the base with Rookwood red and
highlight the tip with Marigold. The eyes, mouth and buttons
are Lamp Black. Shade under the buttons with a little Deep

Midnight Blue. Highlight the eyes, and buttons with dots of
Light Buttermilk. Shade the left side and bottom of the Honey
Brown stripes of the scarf, and both sides of the Honey Brown
stripes of the tie with Burnt Sienna. Highlight the top of
these sections of the scarf and center of the sections of the tie
with Marigold. Shade the bottom of the Rookwood Red stripes
on the scarf and both sides of the Rookwood Red stripes on
the tie and bottom of the heart with Black Plum. Highlight
the top of these sections with Hot Shots Fiery Red. The fringe
of the scarf is lined with Black Plum, then Rookwood Red, and
finally a little Hot Shots Fiery Red.

Finishing:
Outline the design and add stitches on each side of the red
stripes and heart on the scarf with Lamp Black. The
snowflakes are lined and dotted with Light Buttermilk. Varnish
with your favorite product. Tie a string of raffia around a
candle and enjoy. As with all candles, don't leave the candle
burning unattended.

Quilted Stockings

Palette:

DecoArt Americana Paints
Antique White
Burnt Orange
Burnt Sienna
Buttermilk
Country Red
Hauser Dark Green
Honey Brown
Lamp Black
Leaf Green
Light Buttermilk
Marigold
Milk Chocolate
Napa Red
Payne's Grey
Titanium (Snow) White
Uniform Blue
Hot Shots Fiery Red
Hot Shots Thermal Green
Dazzling Metallic Emperor's Gold

Prep:

Sand and seal ornaments, transfer the lines for the cuff and toe, and basecoat the center section with Antique White. Lightly transfer the quilting lines and shade the top of each line (shade all in one direction, allow to dry and shade the other), and around the outside edges with Milk Chocolate. Highlight the center of each square with Light Buttermilk. The stitches along the quilting lines are Emperor's Gold. Transfer the pattern for the design to each stocking and basecoat as follows:

Holly Stocking:
Honey Brown - cuff & toe (dots are Uniform Blue, stitched stars are Napa Red)
Leaf Green - holly leaves
Country Red - berries

Snowman Stocking:
Country Red - cuff & toe (stripes are Leaf Green, lines are Emperor's Gold)
Buttermilk - Snowman

Bell Stocking:
Leaf Green - cuff & toe (large dots are Honey Brown, surrounded by small dots of Uniform Blue, medium dots are Light Buttermilk) and top middle section of the bell
Uniform Blue - top and bottom of bell
Country Red - bottom middle section of the bell
Honey Brown - clapper of bell

Star Stocking:
Uniform Blue - cuff & toe (double line plaid is Honey Brown, hearts are Country Red)
Honey Brown - Star

Painting Instructions:

Holly Stocking: Shade the cuff on both sides and across the bottom, and the toe across the top with Burnt Sienna. Highlight the center top of the cuff and bottom of toe with Marigold. Shade the holly leaves around the outside edge with Hauser Dark Green. Highlight the center with Hot Shots Thermal Green (do this at least twice). Shade the bottom of the berries with Napa Red and highlight the top with Hot Shots Fiery Red. Shade around the outside of the holly, berries, under cuff, and above toe with Milk Chocolate. The stitches along the vein line of the leaves and all blanket stitching around the holly, berries, and bottom of cuff & and top of toe are Lamp Black.

Snowman Stocking: Shade the cuff on both sides and across the bottom and the toe across the top with Napa Red on the red stripes and Hauser Dark Green on the green stripes. Highlight the top of the red stripes on the cuff and bottom of red stripes on the toe with Hot Shots Fiery Red, and the top of the green stripes on the cuff and bottom of green stripes on the toe with Hot Shots Thermal Green. Shade around the outside edge of the snowman with Milk Chocolate. Highlight the center of each part with Titanium White. The nose is basecoated with Burnt Orange, shade the base with Napa Red and highlight the tip with Marigold. Blush the cheeks with Country Red. The eyes, mouth stitches and buttons are Lamp Black. Highlight the top right of the eyes, top of cheeks and top right of buttons with small dots of Titanium White. Shade around the outside of the snowman, under the cuff and above the toe with Milk Chocolate. Blanket stitches around the snowman and bottom of cuff and top of toe are Lamp Black.

Bell Stocking: Shade the cuff on both sides and across the bottom and the toe across the top with Hauser Dark Green. Highlight the top of the cuff and bottom of toe with Hot Shots Thermal Green. Shade the outside of the blue sections of the bell with Payne's Grey, the outside of the green section with Hauser Dark Green, and the outside of the red section with Napa Red. Highlight the center of the blue sections with a brush mix of Uniform Blue + Light Buttermilk. Highlight the center of the green section with Hot Shots Thermal Green and the center of the red section with Hot Shots Fiery Red. Shade the top of the clapper with Burnt Sienna and highlight the bottom of it with Marigold. Shade around the outside of the bell, under the cuff and above the toe with Milk Chocolate. The stitches between the bell sections and blanket stitches around the bell and bottom of cuff and top of toe are Lamp Black.

Star Stocking: Shade the cuff on both sides and across the bottom and the top of the toe with Payne's Grey. Highlight the top center of the cuff and bottom of toe with a brush mix of Uniform Blue + Light Buttermilk. Shade the edges of the star with Burnt Sienna and highlight the center with Marigold. Shade around the outside of the star, under the cuff and above the toe with Milk Chocolate. The blanket stitches around the star, bottom of cuff and top of toe are Lamp Black.

Finishing:

Basecoat the back of the ornaments with Hauser Dark Green. Varnish with your favorite product. Put strings through the holes for hangers.

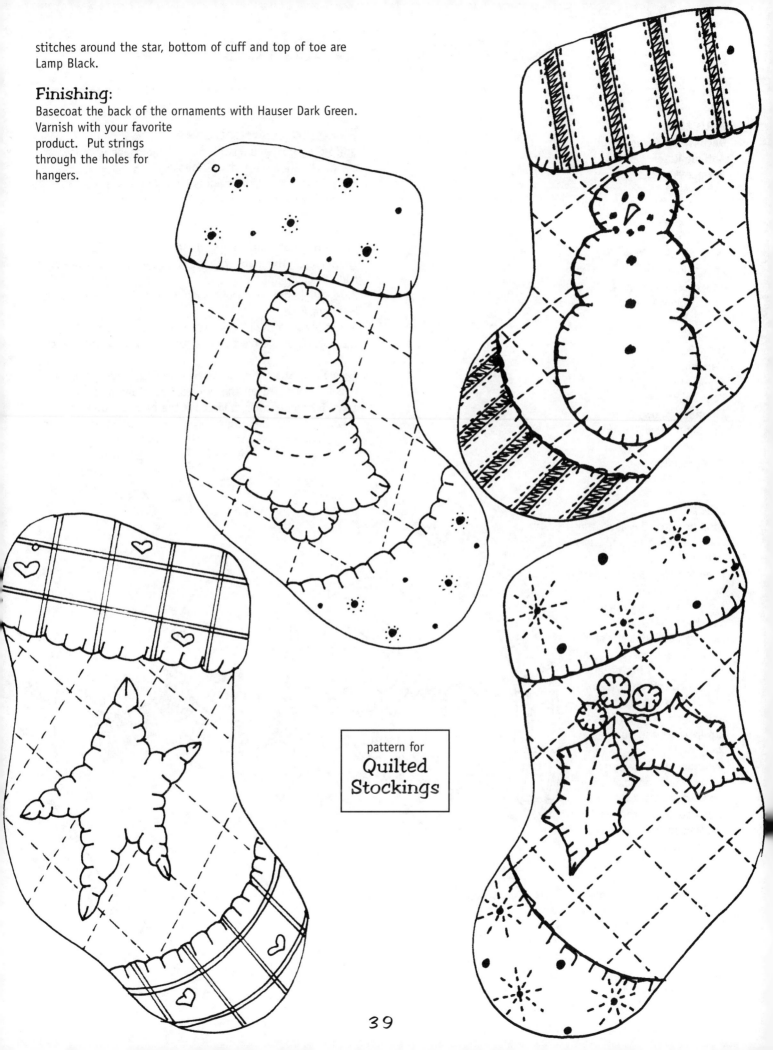

pattern for
Quilted
Stockings

Snowy Patches

Palette:
DecoArt Americana Paints
Antique Rose
Antique White
Avocado
Black Plum
Burnt Sienna
Country Red
Deep Midnight Blue
French Blue Grey
Hauser Dark Green
Hauser Light Green
Honey Brown
Lamp Black
Light Buttermilk
Marigold
Payne's Grey
Rookwood Red
Titanium (Snow) White
Hot Shots Fiery Red

Misc. Supplies:
Kerry Trout's Liquid Shadow

Prep:
Sand and seal the bowl, transfer the main pattern lines and basecoat as follows:
Deep Midnight Blue - Inside of bowl
Light Buttermilk - Stipple Snowmen
Country Red - Hat of right snowman and heart
Honey Brown - Hat of left snowman, cuff and ball on hat of right snowman, and gold blocks on rim (lines are Avocado and Rookwood Red)
Avocado - Cuff, ball and scarf on left snowman (lines on scarf are Marigold) and green blocks on the rim (dots are Marigold)
French Blue Grey - Right snowman's scarf (stripes are Country Red and lines are Honey Brown) and snowflake blocks on the rim (snowflakes are lined & dotted with Light Buttermilk)
Antique White - Tree Blocks on the rim (trees are Avocado, trunks are Burnt Umber)
Rookwood Red - Red Blocks on the rim and outside of the bowl

Painting Instructions:
Quilted Rim: Highlight the centers and shade each side of the blocks around the rim as follows:
Red - Highlight with Hot Shots Fiery Red, line plaid with Light Buttermilk, and shade with Black Plum
Green - Highlight with Hauser Light Green, and shade with Hauser Dark Green
Gold - Highlight with Marigold, and shade with Burnt Sienna
Tree Blocks - Highlight with Light Buttermilk and shade with Milk Chocolate
Blue - Highlight with Light Buttermilk and shade with Deep Midnight Blue
Stitch between the blocks with Lamp Black. Shade around the outside of the bowl against the rim with Liquid Shadow.

Snowmen: Shade the snowmen with Deep Midnight Blue, under the hats, under the scarves, above and below the arms, bottom of arms, and above the heart on the left.
Highlight with Titanium White, center of faces, top of arms, center front of right snowman, and bottoms.
Blush the

cheeks with Antique Rose. Eyes and mouth lines are Lamp Black, noses are Country Red. Highlight the top right of the eyes and top of cheeks with dots of Titanium White.

Left Snowman: Shade the hat with Burnt Sienna, above the cuff and next to the ball. Highlight the top of the hat with Marigold. Shade the cuff with Hauser Dark Green using the chisel edge of your brush to make the rows. Highlight between the rows with Hauser Light Green. Stipple the ball with Hauser Dark Green and then Hauser Light Green. The scarf is shaded with Hauser Dark Green, both sides, bottom of knot, and on the left side of the tie. Highlight with Hauser Light Green, center, top of knot and right side of the tie.

Right Snowman: Shade the hat with Black Plum, above the cuff, and highlight the center top with Hot Shots Fiery Red.

Shade the cuff with Burnt Sienna using the chisel edge of your brush to make the rows. Highlight between the rows with Marigold. Stipple the ball with Burnt Sienna and then Marigold. Shade the scarf with Deep Midnight Blue, both sides, bottom of knot, and left side of the tie. Highlight with Light Buttermilk, center, top of knot and right side of the tie. The heart is shaded with Black Plum all around and highlighted in the center with Hot Shots Fiery Red.

Finishing:
Shade around the inside of the bowl and around the snowmen with Payne's Grey. Outline as necessary with Lamp Black. Dot the snowflakes in the background with Titanium White. Varnish with your favorite product.

Heart Candleholder with Salt Box House

Palette:
DecoArt Americana Paints
Black Plum
Burnt Umber
Deep Midnight Blue
Hauser Dark Green
Hauser Light Green
Lamp Black
Light Avocado
Light Buttermilk
Light French Blue
Rookwood Red
Hot Shots Fiery Red

Prep:
Sand and Seal Candleholder and basecoat surface with Light French Blue. Sand again with Super Film Sanding Sheet. Transfer main painting lines and basecoat as follows:
Light Avocado - Ground
Rookwood Red - House & Chimneys and outside edge of piece
Burnt Umber - Tree Trunks
Lamp Black - Roof of house

Painting Instructions:
Shade around the house, above the ground and around the outside edge of the blue sky with Deep Midnight Blue. Shade the bottom of the ground with Hauser Dark Green, and highlight the top of it with Hauser Light Green. Highlight the top of the roof with Light French Blue. Shade the right side of the side of the house and right side of the front of the house, and under the roof with Black Plum. Highlight the left of the front of the house with Hot Shots Fiery Red. Basecoat the door and windows with Lamp Black. Basecoat the light stripes of the bunting over the door with

Light Buttermilk and the top of it with Deep Midnight Blue. Add a tiny star with Light Buttermilk. Touch a little shading on the light stripes with Burnt Umber. Line the panes of the windows and add a door knob with Light Buttermilk. The trees are lined with Hauser Dark Green, Light Avocado and a little Hauser Light Green.

Finishing:
Outline the house and add the fence with Lamp Black. Varnish with your favorite product. Tie a string of raffia around a candle and enjoy. As with all candles, don't leave the candle burning unattended.

Bunny Patches

Palette:
DecoArt Americana Paints
Antique Gold
Antique Rose
Burnt Umber
Buttermilk
Celery Green
Fawn
Gooseberry Pink
Hauser Medium Green
Lamp Black
Light Buttermilk
Milk Chocolate
Moon Yellow
Pumpkin
Rookwood Red

Prep:
Sand and seal the bowl, transfer main pattern lines and basecoat as follows:
Celery Green - Inside of bowl and green blocks on the rim (double lines are Light Buttermilk)
Buttermilk - Bunny and carrot blocks on the rim (the carrots are Pumpkin & the greenery is stippled with Hauser Medium Green)
Gooseberry Pink - Outside of bowl, pink squares on the rim and bunny's nose
Moon Yellow - Yellow blocks on the rim (dots are Gooseberry Pink)
Fawn - Tan blocks on the rim (dots are Hauser Medium Green)

Painting Instructions:
Quilted Rim: Highlight the centers and shade each side of the blocks around the rim as follows:
Pink - Highlight with a brush mix of Gooseberry Pink + Light Buttermilk, line plaid and shade with Antique Rose
Green - Highlight with Light Buttermilk and shade with Hauser Medium Green
Yellow - Highlight with Light Buttermilk and shade with Antique Gold
Tan - Highlight with Light Buttermilk and shade with Burnt Umber
Carrot Blocks - shade with Milk Chocolate. Shade the base of the carrot with Rookwood Red and highlight the tip with Moon Yellow. Stipple a little Hauser Light Green on the greenery.

Outline carrot with Lamp Black. Stitch between the blocks on the rim with Lamp Black. Shade around the outside of the bowl against the rim with Antique Rose.

Inside of Bowl: Shade around the inside of the bowl and bunny with Hauser Medium Green. Shade the outside edge of the bunny with Milk Chocolate. Highlight the center of face, center of legs and center of body with Light Buttermilk. Highlight the body a second time. Blush the cheek and inside of ear with Gooseberry Pink. Shade the bottom of the nose with Rookwood Red. The eye is Lamp Black. Highlight the front of the eye, top of cheek and top of nose with dots of Light Buttermilk. The whiskers are lined with Light Buttermilk. Mouth stitches are Burnt Umber. Outline the bunny with Lamp Black. Line the wreath around the bunny's neck with Burnt Umber. Highlight some of the sticks of the wreath with lines of Fawn. Outline with Lamp Black. The ribbon is lined with Gooseberry Pink, shaded with Antique Rose bottom of knot and where it crosses over itself. Highlight the outside of the loops with a brush mix of Gooseberry Pink + Light Buttermilk. Outline with Lamp Black.

Finishing:
Varnish with your favorite product.

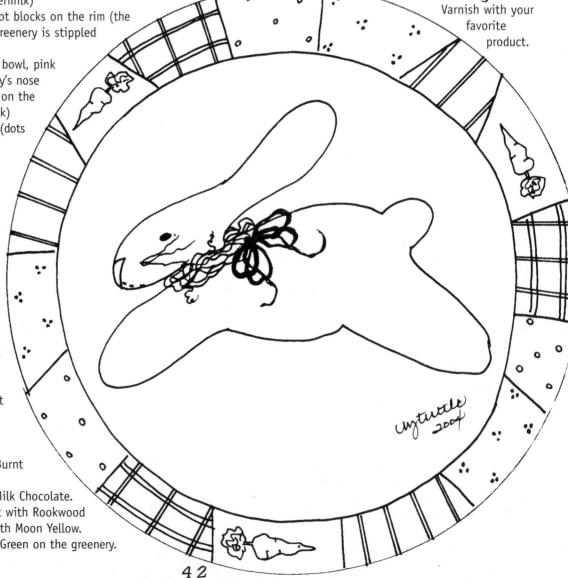

Judy, Judy Garden Angel

Palette:
DecoArt Americana Paints
Antique Gold
Antique Rose
Burnt Sienna
Celery Green
Hauser Dark Green
Hauser Medium Green
Lamp Black
Light Buttermilk
Medium Flesh
Moon Yellow
Rookwood Red
Shading Flesh
Soft Black
Hot Shots Fiery Red

Surface:
Angel Turning from Cupboard Distributing

Misc. Supplies:
DecoArt Multi Purpose Sealer
Yellow Yarn for Hair

Prep:
I removed the wings and birdhouse from the piece for easier painting. I did not use the halo. Sand the wood part and seal. Wash the wings in a 1:1 white vinegar and water solution, allow to dry well and seal. Transfer the main pattern lines and basecoat as follows:
Medium Flesh - Face & hands
Light Buttermilk - Bodice, middle section of the arms, front and back of birdhouse and tulip and plaid patches at the bottom of the dress
Celery Green - Dress, top and long sections of the arms, roof of birdhouse and plaid lines on bottom patches
Moon Yellow - Buttons, sides of birdhouse and yellow patches at the bottom of the dress
Antique Rose - Trim around bodice and top and bottom of patches at the bottom of the dress, tulips and small arm sections
Hauser Dark Green - Tulip leaves and stem

Painting Instructions:
Shade the bottom of the face and on the hands under the sleeves with Shading Flesh. Highlight the center of the face and bottom of the hands with Light Buttermilk. Blush the cheeks with Antique Rose. The eyes and eyebrows are Lamp Black. Add tiny Light Buttermilk highlight dots to the upper right of the eyes and top of cheeks. Shade around the inside of the bodice, top and bottom of middle sections of the sleeves and both sides of the plaid patches with Celery Green. Shade around the outside of the bodice, above the patches, bottom of top arm section, top and bottom of long arm section and center of birdhouse roof with Hauser

Medium Green. Highlight the ends of the birdhouse roof with Light Buttermilk. Shade the inside of the buttons, both sides of the yellow patches, and under the birdhouse roof on the sides with Antique Gold. Highlight the center of the patches with Light Buttermilk. Shade the center and bottom of the tulip petals with Rookwood Red. Highlight the tips with Hot Shots Fiery Red. Sponge the wings with Burnt Sienna and then Soft Black to make them look rusty.

Finishing:
Stitch around the bodice, between arm sections, above, below and between the patches, and around the birdhouse and outline the tulips with Lamp Black. Re-attach wings and birdhouse. Varnish with your favorite product. With the yellow yarn, make tiny bows and glue them to the head.

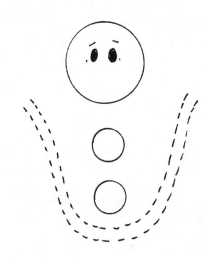

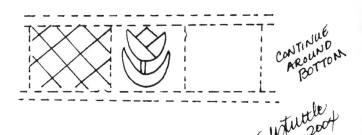

Quilted Welcome

Palette:

DecoArt Americana Paints
Antique White
Avocado
Black Plum
Burnt Sienna
Burnt Umber
Deep Midnight Blue
French Blue Grey
Hauser Dark Green
Honey Brown
Khaki Tan
Lamp Black
Light Buttermilk
Light French Blue
Milk Chocolate
Rookwood Red
Hot Shots Fiery Red
Hot Shots Thermal Green

Misc. Supplies:
JW Fruitwood Wood Stain
American Traditional Stencil - MS121

Prep:
Sand, seal the painting surface and stain the cut edge of the door crown. Basecoat the painting surface with Antique White. Sand again with Super Film Sanding Sheet. Transfer the main pattern lines and basecoat as follows:
Red Patches - Rookwood Red
Green Patches - Avocado
Blue Patches - French Blue Grey
Gold Patches - Honey Brown
Tan Patches - Khaki Tan
Light Patches - Antique White

Painting Instructions:
Highlight the centers of each patch as follows:
Red Patches - Hot Shots Fiery Red
Green Patches - Hot Shots Thermal Green
Blue Patches - Light French Blue
Gold Patches - Marigold
Tan Patches - Antique White
Light Patches - Light Buttermilk
Add the design on each patch as follows:
Red Patches - Plaid is Antique White
Green Patches - Plaid is Deep Midnight Blue, Rookwood Red and French Blue Grey
Blue Patches - Large dots are Light Buttermilk, surrounded by small dots of Deep Midnight Blue & medium dots are Rookwood Red
Gold Patches - Wide lines are Avocado, lines on each side are Rookwood Red and stitches are Light Buttermilk
Tan Patches - Stars are Antique White
Light Patches remain solid

Shade the edges of each patch where they touch one another as follows:
Red Patches - Black Plum
Green Patches - Hauser Dark Green
Blue Patches - Deep Midnight Blue
Gold Patches - Burnt Sienna
Tan Patches - Burnt Umber
Light Patches - Milk Chocolate
Shade all around the inside area with Milk Chocolate.

Finishing:
The lettering and stitches between the patches and around the inside are Lamp Black. Varnish with your favorite product.

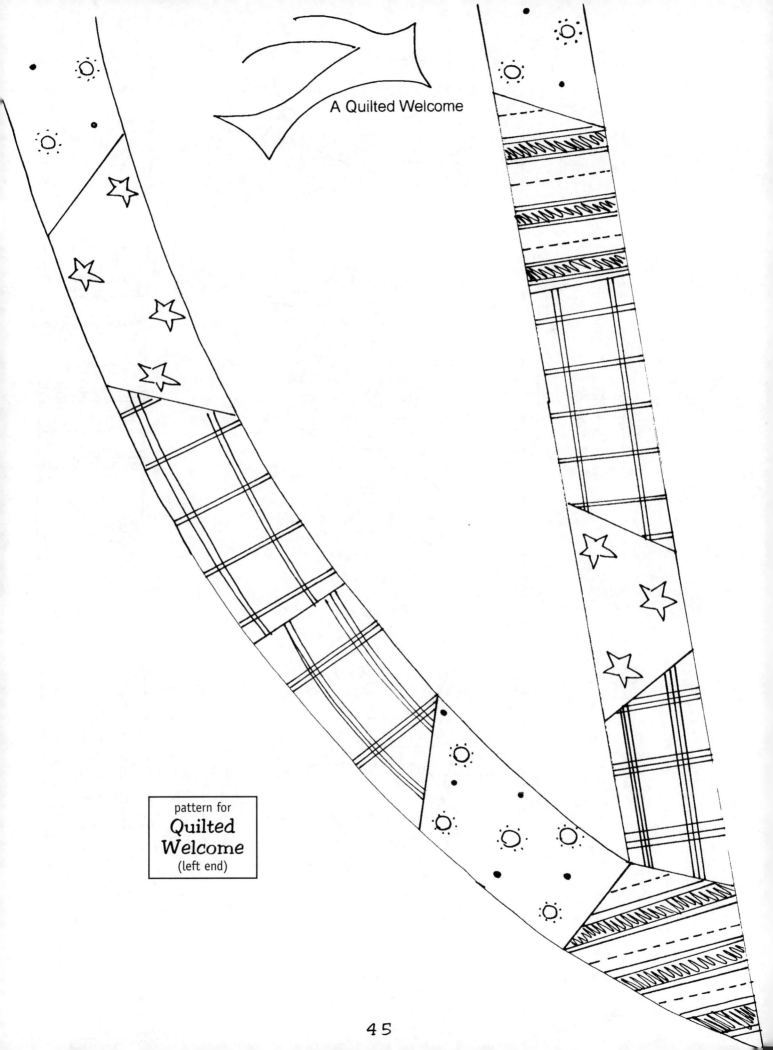

A Quilted Welcome

pattern for
**Quilted
Welcome**
(left end)

pattern for
**Quilted
Welcome**
(middle)

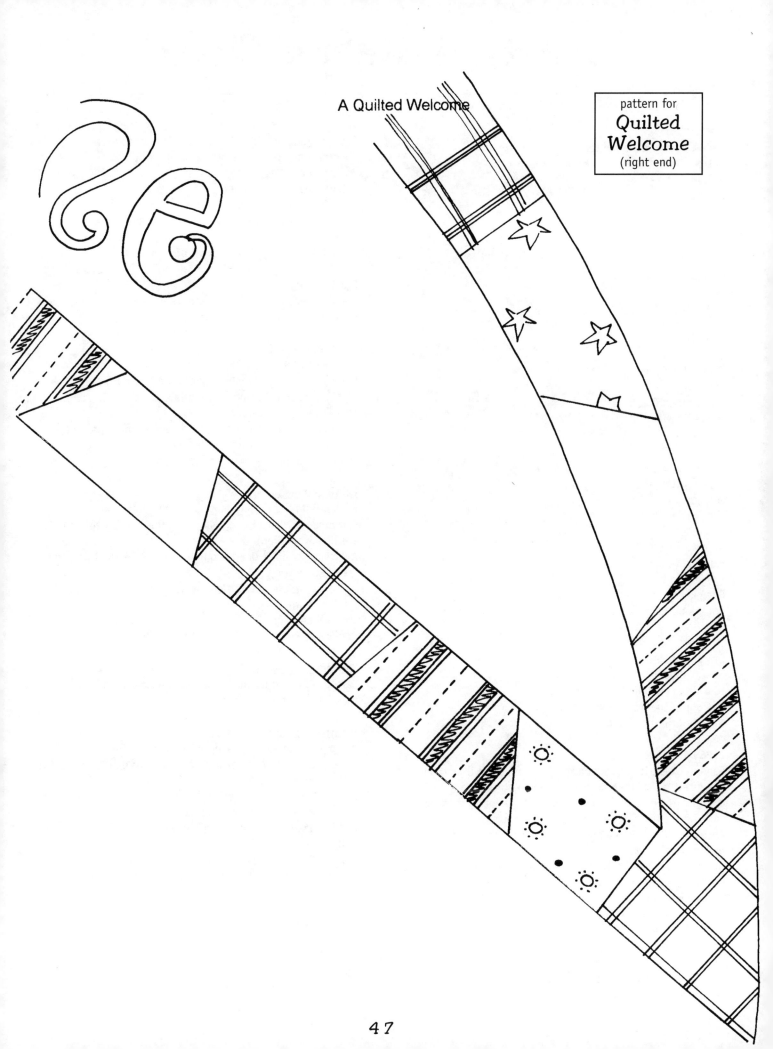

A Quilted Welcome

pattern for
**Quilted
Welcome**
(right end)

47

Crafts 4 Keeps Clock

Palette:
DecoArt Americana Paints
Antique Teal
Antique White
Avocado
Baby Pink
Black Plum
Burnt Sienna
Burnt Umber
Cadmium Yellow
Camel
Celery Green
Country Red
Deep Midnight Blue
Desert Turquoise
French Blue Grey
Graphite
Hauser Dark Green
Honey Brown
Khaki Tan
Lamp Black
Leaf Green
Light Buttermilk
Marigold
Milk Chocolate
Napa Red
Neutral Grey
Pansy Lavender
Payne's Grey
Pumpkin
Rookwood Red
Soft Black
Titanium (Snow) White
Uniform Blue
Winter Blue
Hot Shots Fiery Red
Hot Shots Thermal Green
Hot Shots Torrid Orange

Prep:
Sand and seal the clock and insert (I painted a design on the insert rather than using the printed clock face that comes with the piece) and basecoat the painting surfaces with Antique White, and the outside and inside trim with Rookwood Red. Shade around the outside and inside edges of the clock with Burnt Umber. Transfer the main pattern lines to the clock. (The scrap booking design is about 1:00 on the clock, the pin cushion is about 4:00, the quilting basket is at 6:00, the knitting is at about 8:00 and the painting design is about 11:00.) Basecoat as follows:

Scrap Booking Design:
Uniform Blue - box
Graphite - scissor bottoms
Leaf Green - handles & screw on bottom scissors
Pansy Lavender - handles and screw on scissors in box

Light Buttermilk - glue bottle and sticker cards (hearts are Country Red and Stars are Marigold), and label on box
Country Red - pen, glue bottle lid & stripes
Winter Blue - back paper
Celery Green - next paper
Baby Pink - next paper
Camel - front paper and pencil (top and bottom are Graphite)
Marigold - trim around label on box

Pin Cushion:
Country Red - pin cushion & strawberry emery
Leaf Green - leaves and string

Quilting Basket:
Milk Chocolate - basket
Pumpkin - scissor handles (blades are Neutral Grey)
Light Buttermilk - bands around fabric
Leaf Green - top floss
Country Red - bottom floss (bands around floss are Deep Midnight Blue with Marigold bands)
Marigold - tape measure (end is Graphite)

Fabric bundles L to R:
French Blue Grey - large dots are Light Buttermilk surrounded by small Deep Midnight Blue dots, medium dots are Rookwood Red)
Avocado - plaid is Deep Midnight Blue, Rookwood Red and French Blue Grey
Khaki Tan - stars are Antique White
Honey Brown - lines are Avocado and Rookwood Red and stitches are Light Buttermilk
Rookwood Red - plaid is Light Buttermilk

Yarn Ball & Needles:
Camel - knitting needles (ends are Neutral Grey)
Deep Midnight Blue - yarn

Painting Design:
Antique White - crock (band is French Blue Grey)
Neutral Grey - ferrules of brushes, blade of palette knife, top and end of paint tube
Honey Brown - ruler, brush bristles, top of paint bottle
Milk Chocolate - palette knife handle
Light Buttermilk - paint tube (stripes are Graphite and paint is Burnt Sienna)
French Blue Grey - paint in bottle
Avocado - paint bottle label (stripes and heart are Country Red)
Graphite - brush handle on left
Antique Teal - middle brush handle
Country Red - brush handle on right

Clock Face:
Lamp Black - numbers

Honey Brown - 1:00 and 7:00 buttons
Avocado - 2:00 and 8:00 buttons
French Blue Grey - 4:00 and 10:00 buttons
Rookwood Red - 5:00 and 11:00 buttons

Painting Instructions:

Scrap Booking Design:
Stipple the box with Light Buttermilk. Shade with Payne's Grey, under the lip, top of the lip and down both sides. Highlight the bottom of the lip with Light Buttermilk. Shade the trim around the label at the corners with Burnt Sienna and highlight the center of each side with Marigold. Shade the label with Soft Black on each side and highlight the center with Titanium White. The "2004" is Neutral Grey. Shade the bottom blades of the scissors with Lamp Black, and highlight the top blades with Light Buttermilk. Shade the handles of both scissors with Payne's Grey, next to the blades, bottom of each handle and bottom of the screws. Highlight the top of the handles and screw of the green scissors with Hot Shots Thermal Green, and the top of the handles and screw of the purple scissors with a brush mix of Pansy Lavender + Light Buttermilk. The design on the green scissor blade is Light Buttermilk. Shade the pen with Napa Red at the bottom, inside and under the cap. Highlight down the center with Hot Shots Fiery Red. The clip is Neutral Grey. Shade the bottom of the green paper with Avocado, the bottom of the pink paper with Napa Red, the bottom of the yellow paper with Burnt Sienna, and the left side and bottom of the blue paper with Payne's Grey. Highlight the tops of all of the papers with Light Buttermilk. Shade the glue bottle with Soft Black on both sides. Shade the bottom of the cap and sides of the stripes with Napa Red. Highlight the tip of the cap and center of the stripes with Hot Shots Fiery Red. Line the lid with Soft Black. Shade the left side of the sticker cards with Soft Black. Shade across the bottom of all items in the box with Soft Black to set them inside. Shade the bottom of the pencil with Burnt Sienna and highlight with a line of Light Buttermilk down the center. Shade around the outside and under the design with Burnt Umber, and outline as necessary with Lamp Black.

Pin Cushion:
Shade the pin cushion with Napa Red, outside edges, both sides of divider string, and under the leaves, and on the strawberry, both sides and under the leaves. Shade again with Black Plum, under the leaves and in the holes where the pins will go. Highlight the center section of the pin cushion and bottom of the strawberry with Hot Shots Fiery Red. Shade the base of the leaves and on the string where it crosses over itself and top and bottom with Hauser Dark Green. Highlight the tips of the leaves and loops of the string with Hot Shots Thermal Green. Basecoat the pins with Neutral Grey, shade top and bottom with Graphite and highlight with a thin line of Light Buttermilk down the center of each. The ball ends are Marigold shaded on the bottom with Burnt Sienna and highlighted on the top with a dot of Light Buttermilk. Shade around the outside and under the design with Burnt Umber and outline as necessary with Lamp Black.

Quilting Basket:
Wash the deep insides of the basket with Burnt Umber. Shade the slats of the basket with Burnt Umber, on the outer edges, bottom of the top band, and where they go under one another. Highlight the center of top band, and center of each slat with Marigold. The grain lines are Soft Black. Shade the bottom of the scissor handles with Napa Red and highlight the tops with Hot Shots Torrid Orange. Shade the bottom of each blade with Graphite and highlight the top of the bottom blade with Light Buttermilk. The screw is a dot of Graphite outlined with Lamp Black. Shade the blue fabric with Payne's Grey, inside the folds and across the bottom next to the band. Highlight the top of the folds with Light Buttermilk. Shade the green fabric with Hauser Dark Green, inside the folds and across the bottom next to the band. Highlight the top of the folds with Hot Shots Thermal Green. Shade the tan fabric with Burnt Umber, inside the folds and across the bottom next to the band. Highlight the top of the folds with Antique White. Shade the gold fabric with Burnt Sienna, inside the folds and at the top and bottom of the band. Highlight the top of the folds with Marigold. Shade the red fabric with Black Plum, inside the folds and across the bottom next to the band. Highlight the top of the folds with Hot Shots Fiery Red. The bands are shaded on both sides with Soft Black, and the center is highlighted with Titanium White. Shade across the bottom of all of the fabric where it goes into the basket with Soft Black. Shade the green floss with Hauser Dark Green, next to the band, and at the fold. Highlight with lines of Hot Shots Thermal Green. Shade the red floss with Napa Red, next to the band, at the folds, and on the string where it bends. Highlight with lines of Hot Shots Fiery Red. Shade between the bands with Payne's Grey. Shade the tape measure with Burnt Sienna, at the top, in the curl, under the curl and above the end. Highlight with Cadmium Yellow on the top of the curl and in the center above the end. Shade around the tape measure where it touches the basket with Soft Black. The lines are Lamp Black. Shade around and under the design with Burnt Umber and outline as necessary with Lamp Black.

Yarn Ball & Needles:
Shade the knitting needles with Burnt Sienna, next to the ends and where they go into and come out of the yarn ball. Highlight the tips and center of the top with Light Buttermilk. Shade the ends with Graphite and highlight the edges with Light Buttermilk. Shade the yarn ball with Payne's Grey to separate strands of yarn, and highlight with lines of Desert Turquoise. Shade around and under the design with Burnt Umber and outline as necessary with Lamp Black.

Painting Design:
Shade the crock with Burnt Umber, under the rim, down both sides, right of the paint tube, and inside. Deepen the shading under the rim, next to the paint tube and inside with Soft Black. Highlight the center of the rim and crock with Light Buttermilk. Shade the top and bottom of the light parts of the paint tube with Soft Black. Highlight the center of these parts, center of the rim and top of the dark

parts with Titanium White. Shade the sides of the rim with Graphite. Shade the paint coming from the tube with Soft Black, along the bottom and where it comes out of the tube. Highlight with dabs of Mairgold. Shade the paint bottle lid with Burnt Sienna, top and bottom of the lid, bottom of the flip top, and down both sides of the lid. Line the edge of the lid with Burnt Sienna. Highlight the tip of the flip top, top of the lid, and top edge of the lid with Marigold. Shade the both sides of the paint bottle with Payne's Grey. Shade the bottom of the heart with Napa Red and highlight the top of the heart and center of the red stripes with Hot Shots Fiery Red. Shade the ferrules of the brushes on both sides with Graphite, and highlight the center of each with Light Buttermilk. Shade the palette knife with Graphite, bottom of blade, side of blade, and top and bottom of shaft. Highlight the tip of the blade with Light Buttermilk. Shade the sides of the handle with Soft Black and highlight the center with Marigold. Grain lines are Lamp Black. Shade all brush bristles with Burnt Sienna at the base, and highlight with Marigold at the top. Pull some lines of Burnt Sienna to show bristles. Shade the handle of the fan brush with

Lamp Black under the ferrule, and highlight with a line of Light Buttermilk down the center. Shade the handle of the flat brush with Payne's Grey, under the ferrule and down the left side and highlight the right side with a brush mix of Antique Teal + Light Buttermilk. Shade the handle of the red brush under the ferrule with Napa Red and highlight the center with Hot Shots Fiery Red. Shade the right side of the ruler with Soft Black and highlight the left side with Marigold. Add the lines and numbers with Lamp Black. Shade across the bottom of all items in the crock with Soft Black. Shade around and under the design with Burnt Umber and outline as necessary with Lamp Black.

Clock Face:
Shade and highlight the buttons as follows:
Gold Buttons - Shade around the inside and at the bottom with Burnt Sienna and highlight the center and top right with Marigold.

Green Buttons - Shade around the inside and at the bottom with Hauser Dark Green and highlight the center and top right with Hot Shots Thermal Green

Blue Buttons - Shade around the

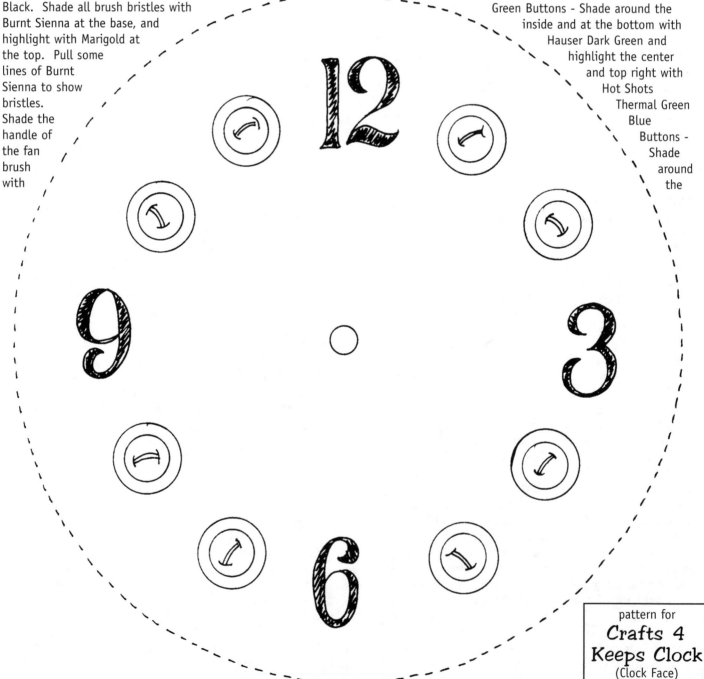

pattern for
Crafts 4 Keeps Clock
(Clock Face)

inside and at the bottom with Deep Midnight Blue and highlight the center and top right with Light Buttermilk. Red Buttons - Shade around the inside and at the bottom with Black Plum and highlight the center and top right with Hot Shots Fiery Red.

Line the thread with Antique White and shade the ends with Soft Black.

Place the face into the clock, and draw a chalk line where it touches the clock. Remove and shade to the inside of the chalk line around the face with Burnt Umber.

Finishing:

Varnish the clock and face with your favorite product. Glue the face into the clock and add the clock works and hands.

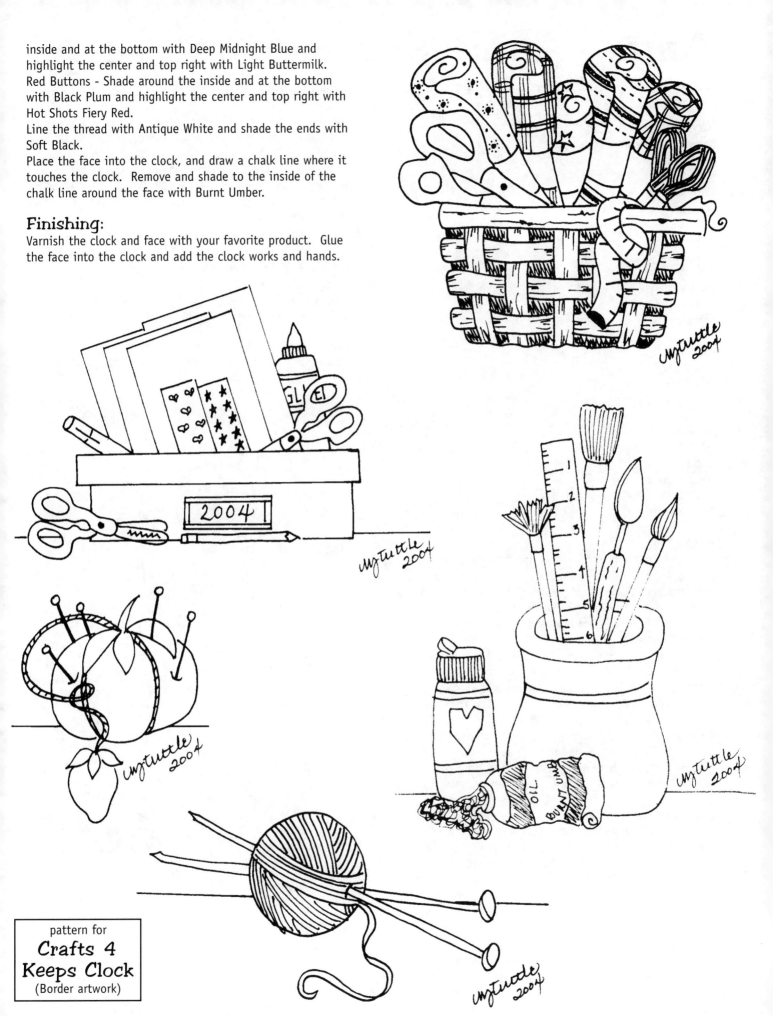

pattern for
Crafts 4 Keeps Clock
(Border artwork)

Annie, Annie Summertime Angel

Palette:
DecoArt Americana Paints
Antique Rose
Antique White
Black Plum
Burnt Sienna
Burnt Umber
Fawn
French Blue Grey
Lamp Black
Light Buttermilk
Medium Flesh
Milk Chocolate
Payne's Grey
Rookwood Red
Shading Flesh
Soft Black
Hot Shots Fiery Red

Surface:
Angel Turning from Cupboard Distributing

Misc. Supplies:
DecoArt Multi Purpose Sealer
Red yarn for hair

Prep:
I removed the wings and watering can from the piece for easier painting. I did not use the halo. Sand the wood parts and seal. Wash the wings in a 1:1 white vinegar and water solution, allow to dry well and seal.
Transfer the main painting lines and basecoat as follows:
Medium Flesh - Face & hands
Antique White - Apron, top and bottom bands on watering can (stripes are Rookwood Red), light patches around the apron bottom and top & longest arm sections
Fawn - Bodice, middle arm section and bottom of the dress (the stripes and stitches are Rookwood Red)
Rookwood Red - Red patches on apron bottom, smallest arm section, heart on bodice, and top & spout on watering can
French Blue Grey - Blue patches on apron bottom (star is Light Buttermilk), center, handle and spout on watering can.

Painting Instructions:
Shade around the bottom of the head and on the hands under the sleeves with Shading Flesh. Highlight the center of the face and bottom of the hands with Light Buttermilk. Blush the cheeks with Antique Rose. The nose and mouth line are Rookwood Red, eyes and stitches are Lamp Black. Shade the bottom of the nose with Black Plum and highlight the top with Hot Shots Fiery Red. Add Light Buttermilk highlight dots top right of eyes and top of cheeks. Shade the on the apron around the bodice and around the bottom, both sides of the light patches at the bottom, top and bottom of long arm sections, and bottom of top arm section

with Milk Chocolate. Highlight the center of the patches with Light Buttermilk. Shade the bodice, under the apron, and top and bottom of middle arm sections with Soft Black. Shade the bottom of the heart, and both sides of the red patches on the apron with Black Plum. Highlight the top of the heart and center of the patches with Hot Shots Fiery Red. Shade both sides of the blue patches on the apron and top and bottom of the blue section on the watering can with Payne's Grey. Sponge the wings with Burnt Sienna, and then Soft Black to make them look rusty.

Finishing:
Stitch with Lamp Black, around bodice, between arm sections, above, below and between patches on apron. Re-attach wings and watering can. Varnish with your favorite product. With the red yarn, make tiny bows and glue them to the head.

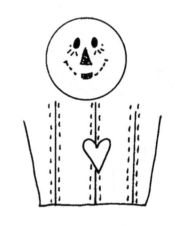

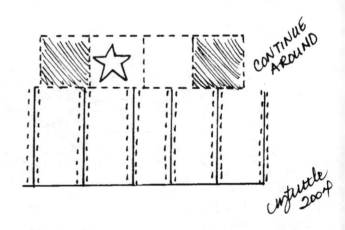

CONTINUE AROUND

The Flag

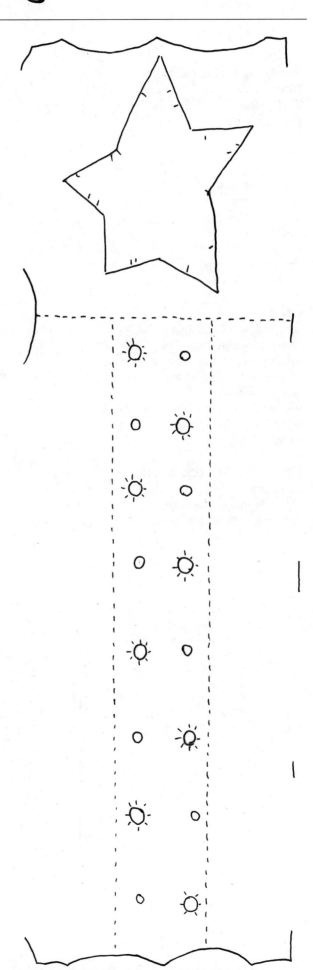

Palette:

DecoArt Americana Paints
Antique White
Black Plum
Burnt Umber
Deep Midnight Blue
Desert Turquoise
Lamp Black
Light Buttermilk
Payne's Grey
Rookwood Red
Titanium (Snow) White
Hot Shots Fiery Red

Misc. Supplies:
DecoArt Multi Purpose Sealer

Prep:

Sand and seal wood piece. Sand again with Super Film
Sanding Sheet and basecoat as follows:
Light Buttermilk - Star
Antique White - Center stripe (large dots are Rookwood Red,
surrounded by small dots of Deep Midnight Blue; medium
dots are Light Buttermilk) and sides top and bottom of piece
Rookwood Red - Top and bottom stripes
Deep Midnight Blue - Field of flag

Painting Instructions:

Highlight the center of the star with Titanium White. Shade
all around the star with Burnt Umber. Shade the left side of
the field and around the outside of the star with Payne's
Grey. Highlight the right side of the field with Desert
Turquoise. Outline the star and add crazy stitches with
Lamp Black. Shade both ends of the red stripes with Black
Plum. Highlight the center of the red stripes with Hot Shots
Fiery Red. Shade both ends of the light stripes with Burnt
Umber. Shade around the top and ends of the piece with
Burnt Umber.

Finishing:

Add stitches between the stripes and on right edge of the
field and crazy stitches around the star with Lamp Black.
Varnish with your favorite product. Never leave a candle
burning unattended.

53

Heart Candleholder with Raggedy

Palette:
DecoArt Americana Paints
Antique Rose
Black Plum
Burnt Umber
Country Red
Fawn
Lamp Black
Light Buttermilk
Medium Flesh
Rookwood Red
Shading Flesh
Soft Black
Titanium (Snow) White
Hot Shots Fiery Red

Prep:
Sand and Seal Candleholder and basecoat surface with Fawn.
Sand again with Super Film Sanding Sheet. Transfer main
pattern lines and basecoat as follows:
Deep Midnight Blue - Stripes & stitches in background and
edge of piece
Medium Flesh - Head and neck
Light Buttermilk - Apron
Rookwood Red - Dress

Painting Instructions:
Shade top of head and under chin on neck with Shading
Flesh. Highlight the center of the face with Light
Buttermilk. Blush the cheeks with Antique Rose. Basecoat

the nose and mouth line with Rookwood Red. Shade the
bottom of the nose and both sides of mouth line with Black
Plum. Highlight the top of the nose and center of mouth
line with Hot Shots Fiery Red. Outline the nose & mouth
line, fill in the eyes and add stitches under eyes and mouth
with Lamp Black. Highlight the top right of the eyes and
top of the cheeks with dots of Light Buttermilk.

Shade the apron above the ruffle on the straps, and above
and below the gather line with Soft Black. Highlight the
top of the straps, top of the ruffle and center of the bottom
of the apron with Titanium White. The stitches and gather
lines are lined with Lamp Black. Highlight the center of the
sleeves and center of bodice of the dress with Hot Shots
Fiery Red. Line the plaid on the dress with Light Buttermilk.
Shade both sides of the sleeves and inside the bodice with
Black Plum.

Finishing:
Shade around the design and around the outside edge of the
candleholder with Burnt Umber. Outline design with Lamp
Black. The hair is lined with Country Red. When dry, shade
the loops with Black Plum where they go into the head and
cross over each other. Highlight the ends of some of the
loops with Hot Shots Fiery Red. Outline hair with Lamp
Black. Varnish with your favorite product. Tie a string of
raffia around a candle and enjoy. As with all candles, don't
leave the candle burning unattended.

Flag House Note Holder

Palette:
DecoArt Americana Paints
Black Plum
Burnt Sienna
Burnt Umber
Deep Midnight Blue
Fawn
Honey Brown
Lamp Black
Light Buttermilk
Light French Blue
Marigold
Mississippi Mud
Payne's Grey
Rookwood Red
Titanium (Snow) White
Uniform Blue
Hot Shots Fiery Red

Misc. Supplies:
American Traditional Stencil MS 121

Prep:
Sand and seal piece, sand again with Super Film Sanding Sheet. Transfer main pattern lines and basecoat as follows:
Light Buttermilk - light stripes on the flag
Rookwood Red - red stripes on the flag, chimneys, cut edges and bottom of piece
Fawn - background & door (stars are Mississippi Mud) and outside sashing
Uniform Blue - roof (plaid is Light Buttermilk)
Honey Brown - front triangle of house (dots are Rookwood Red, Deep Midnight Blue and Light Buttermilk)
Light French Blue - front of house (lines are Uniform Blue & stitches are Light Buttermilk)
Deep Midnight Blue - field of flag (stars are Light Buttermilk), sashing corners and back and sides of piece (stars are Honey Brown)

Painting Instructions:
Shade the sashing against the corner squares, around the outside of the background, and top and bottom of the door with Burnt Umber. Highlight the centers of the sashing with Light Buttermilk. Shade the ends of the light stripes on the flag with Burnt Umber and highlight the center with Titanium White. Shade the ends of the red stripes on the flag and the bottom of the chimneys with Black Plum. Highlight the center of the red stripes on the flag and to of the chimneys with Hot Shots Fiery Red. Shade the left side of the field and inside edges of the corners with Payne's Grey. Highlight the right side of the field with Light French Blue. Shade the sides and bottom of the roof with Deep Midnight Blue and highlight the center top of the roof with Light French Blue. Shade around the house front with Uniform Blue and highlight above the door with Light

Buttermilk. Highlight the center of the triangle with Marigold and shade around the triangle with Burnt Sienna. The stars at the top are shaded on the bottom left with Burnt Sienna and highlighted on the upper right with Marigold. The piece is outlined with stitches of Lamp Black.

Finishing:
Varnish with your favorite product.

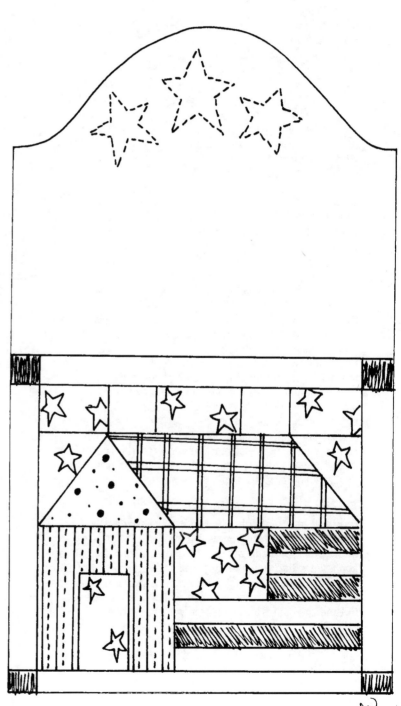

USA Apple Patches

*Raffia Bow Pattern
on next page.

Palette:

DecoArt Americana Paints
Antique White
Black Plum
Burnt Umber
Deep Midnight Blue
Desert Turquoise
Fawn
French Blue Grey
Hauser Dark Green
Lamp Black
Light Avocado
Light Buttermilk
Milk Chocolate
Mississippi Mud
Payne's Grey
Rookwood Red
Titanium (Snow) White
Hot Shots Fiery Red

Misc. Supplies:
Kerry Trout's Liquid Shadow

Prep:
Sand and seal the bowl, transfer the main pattern lines and basecoat as follows:
Fawn - Inside of bowl and apple blocks on the rim (apples are Rookwood Red, leaves are Light Avocado and stems are Mississippi Mud)
Light Buttermilk - Light stripes and star on the apple, and light blocks on the rim
Rookwood Red - red stripes on the apple and red blocks on the rim, and outside of the bowl
Deep Midnight Blue - Field of the apple and star blocks on the rim (stars are Light Buttermilk)
Light Avocado - Leaf
Mississippi Mud - Apple stem
French Blue Grey - Blue blocks on the rim (large dots are Deep Midnight Blue, surrounded by small dots of Rookwood Red, medium dots are Light Buttermilk)

Painting Instructions:
Quilted Rim: Highlight the centers and shade each side of the blocks around the rim as follows:
Apple Blocks - shade with Burnt Umber. Shade bottom of apple with Black Plum and highlight the top with Hot Shots Fiery Red. Shade the bottom of the leaf with Hauser Dark Green and highlight the tip with Hauser Light Green.
Outline the apple, leaf and stem with Lamp Black.
Red - Highlight with Hot Shots Fiery Red, line the plaid with Light Buttermilk and shade with Black Plum.
Light - Highlight with Titanium White, the lines and stitches are Rookwood Red, and shade with Milk Chocolate
Blue - Highlight with Light Buttermilk and shade with Deep Midnight Blue
Star Blocks - Highlight with Desert Turquoise and shade with Payne's Grey

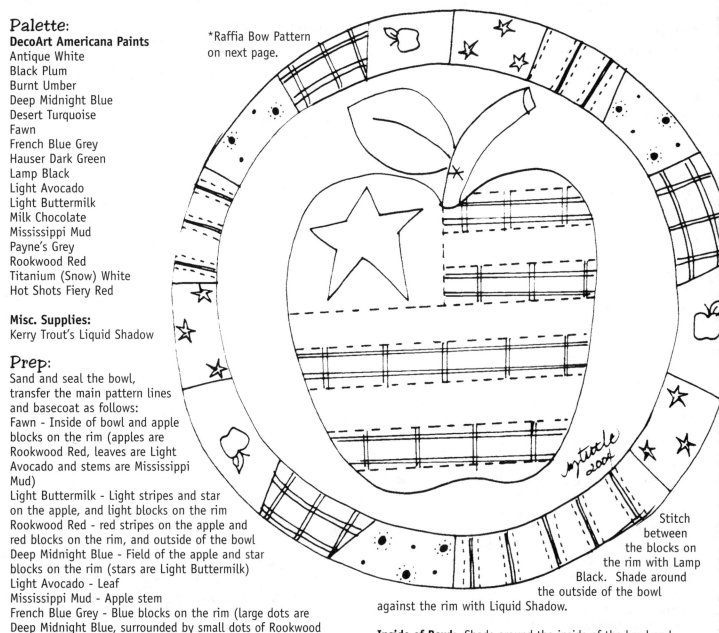

Stitch between the blocks on the rim with Lamp Black. Shade around the outside of the bowl against the rim with Liquid Shadow.

Inside of Bowl: Shade around the inside of the bowl and around the apple with Burnt Umber. Shade the ends of the light stripes and bottom of the star with Milk Chocolate. Highlight the center of the stripes and top of the star with Titanium White. Highlight the centers of the red stripes with Hot Shots Fiery Red, line the plaid with Light Buttermilk, and shade the ends with Black Plum. Stitches between the stripes, around star and field are Lamp Black. Shade the stem at the bottom and inside the top with Burnt Umber. Highlight under the top of the stem with Antique White. Shade the leaf at the base and top of the vein with Hauser Dark Green. Highlight the tip of the leaf and bottom of the vein with Hauser Light Green. Outline apple, stem and leaf with Lamp Black. The raffia is lined with Antique White. Shade the bottom of the knot and where it crosses over itself with Burnt Umber. Highlight the top of the knot, outside of the loops and ends of the ties with Light Buttermilk. Outline with Lamp Black.

Finishing:
Varnish with your favorite product.

*Raffia Bow Pattern
for **USA Apple
Patches** and
Pumpkin Patches

Heart Candleholder with Pumpkin

Palette:

DecoArt Americana Paints
Antique White
Burnt Orange
Burnt Sienna
Burnt Umber
Fawn
Hauser Dark Green
Hauser Light Green
Lamp Black
Light Avocado
Light Buttermilk
Marigold
Rookwood Red
Soft Black
Hot Shots Torrid Orange

Prep:

Sand and Seal the candleholder and basecoat the painting surface with Fawn. Sand again with Super Film Sanding Sheet. Transfer main pattern lines and basecoat as follows:
Burnt Orange - Pumpkin and edge of piece
Marigold - Sunflower
Light Avocado - leaves
Burnt Umber - Stem and sunflower center

Painting Instructions:

Shade the pumpkin with Rookwood Red, outside edges and both sides of seam lines. Highlight the center of each section with Hot Shots Torrid Orange. Shade the base of the leaves with Hauser Dark Green and highlight the tips with Hauser Light Green. Shade the bottom of the sunflower with Burnt Sienna and highlight the top with Light Buttermilk. Shade the base of the stem and bottom of the center of the sunflower with Soft Black.

Finishing:

Shade around the design and outside edge of the candleholder with Burnt Umber. Shade a second time under the pumpkin to deepen a bit. Outline the design and add stitches between sections of pumpkin, around center of sunflower and around the outside edge with Lamp Black. The raffia tie is lined with Antique White. Shade next to the knot, bottom of the knot, and where the loops cross over each other with Burnt Umber. Highlight the outside of the loops, top of the knot, and ends of the ties with Light Buttermilk. Varnish with your favorite product. Tie a string of raffia around a candle and enjoy. As will all candles, don't leave the candle burning unattended.

Pumpkin Patches

Palette:

DecoArt Americana Paints
Antique White
Burnt Orange
Buttermilk
Camel
Hauser Dark Green
Hauser Light Green
Lamp Black
Light Avocado
Milk Chocolate
Mississippi Mud
Pumpkin
Raw Sienna
Rookwood Red
Soft Black
Hot Shots Torrid Orange

Misc. Supplies:
Kerry Trout's Liquid
Shadow

Prep:

Sand and seal the bowl,
transfer the main pattern
lines and basecoat as
follows:
Camel - Inside of bowl and 3
blocks on the rim
Buttermilk - Leaf Blocks on the
rim (leaves are Pumpkin)
Pumpkin - Pumpkin and 3 blocks on
the rim
Light Avocado - Leaf and 3 blocks on the
rim
Burnt Orange - Button and 3 blocks on the rim
Mississippi Mud - Stem

*Raffia Bow Pattern
on previous page.

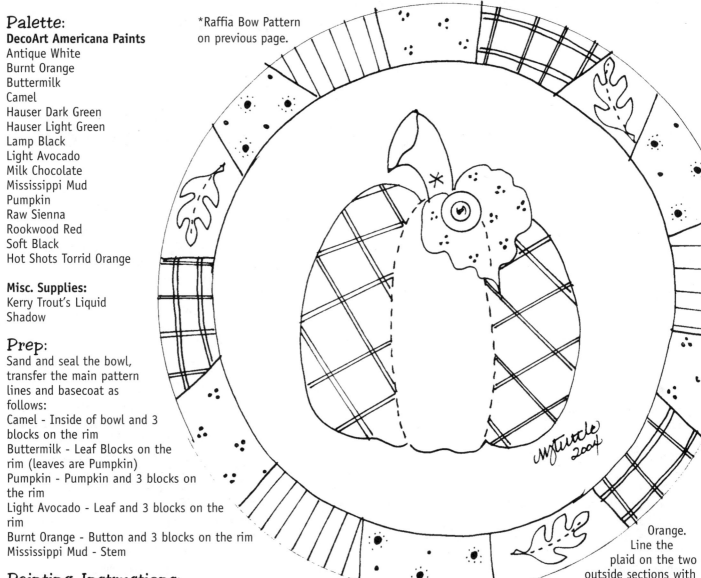

Painting Instructions:

Quilted Rim: Highlight the centers and shade each side of
the blocks around the rim as follows:
Camel - Highlight with Buttermilk, large dots are Burnt
Orange surrounded by small Light Avocado ones, and medium
dots are Buttermilk, shade with Raw Sienna.
Leaf Blocks - Shade with Milk Chocolate, shade the base of
the leaf with Rookwood Red and highlight the tip with Hot
Shots Torrid Orange. Outline and stitches are Lamp Black.
Pumpkin - Highlight with Hot Shots Torrid Orange, plaid is
Burnt Orange, shade with Burnt Orange.
Light Avocado - Highlight with Hauser Light Green, dots are
Camel, shade with Hauser Dark Green.
Burnt Orange - Highlight with Hot Shots Torrid Orange, lines
are Buttermilk, shade with Rookwood Red.
Stitches between the blocks are Lamp Black. Shade around
the outside of the bowl next to the rim with Liquid Shadow.

Inside of Bowl: Shade around the inside of the bowl and
around the pumpkin with Raw Sienna. Highlight the center
of each section of the pumpkin with Hot Shots Torrid

Orange.
Line the
plaid on the two
outside sections with
Burnt Orange. Shade the
pumpkin with Burnt Orange, on the
outside edges, both sides of the seam lines, and under the
leaf. Shade again with Rookwood Red, on the outside of the
center section and under the leaf. The stitches are Lamp
Black. Shade the stem with Soft Black, at the bottom, and
inside the top. Highlight against the top with Antique
White. Shade the leaf with Hauser Dark Green, at the base
and under the button. Highlight the tip of the leaf with
Hauser Light Green. The vein is stitched with Lamp Black.
Shade the button around the inside and bottom with
Rookwood Red and highlight the upper right with Hot Shots
Torrid Orange. The thread is lined with Buttermilk. Outline
the pumpkin, leaf and stem with Lamp Black. The raffia is
lined with Antique White. Shade with Milk Chocolate, at the
bottom of the knot and where the bow crosses over itself.
Highlight the top of the knot, outside of the loops and ends
of the ties with Buttermilk. Outline with Lamp Black.

Finishing:

Varnish with your favorite product.